pipes & strings

Books by Bill Ballantine

Wild Tigers & Tame Fleas
Kangaroos in the Kitchen
Horses & Their Bosses
Nobody Loves a Cockroach
High West
The Piano
The Violin
The Flute
Clown Alley
Pipes & Strings

pipes & strings

by Bill Ballantine

with line drawings by the author

Richardson & Steirman
New York, New York

The Author wishes to thank:

Helen Thurber for her kind permission to quote from
The World of John McNulty by James Thurber.

Donald Henahan for permission to quote from "This Ageless Hero,
Rubenstein," originally published in The New York Times Magazine.

ISBN 0-931933-15-3

Library of Congress Catalog Number: 86-061797

Distributed to the trade by:
Kampmann & Company, Inc.
New York, New York

Printed and bound in Canada by Gagne Printing

a musical vaudeville

in four acts & an olio

To JOE and MARIAN McKENNON

Contents

"It would be very easy to do these things by traditional methods. But this way I can engage the mind of the viewer in a direction he hadn't foreseen and make him discover things he had forgotten."

Pablo Picasso   **(1881–1973)**
  Spanish modernist painter.
  Discussing his creation of sculpture from found objects.
  Françoise Gilot and Carlton Lake, *Life With Picasso*, 1964

Clay fragment: Peruvian Tiahuanaco . . . Collection of Dr. Eduard Gaffron. Courtesy, The Art Institute of Chicago.

piping

"The wind is one of my sounds. A lonely sound, perhaps, but soothing. Everybody should have his personal sounds to listen for — sounds that will make him exhilarated and alive, or quiet and calm. . . . As a matter of fact, one of the greatest sounds of all — and to me it *is* a sound — is utter, complete silence."

Walter Savage Landor   (1775–1864)
English author, poet.

The earliest mention of a vertical flute is on a prehistoric slate from the fourth millenium B.C. to allure wild game. That flute, called a *ma't*, was about three feet in length.

"I sometimes think that the most plaintive ditty has brought a fuller joy and of longer duration to its composer than the conquest of Persia to the Macedonian."

André Kostelanetz   (1901–1980)
Symphonic conductor.
New York *Journal-American*
8 Feb. 1955

Pottery shard found at Elam, in Numma (the highlands) of northern Persia (Iran)

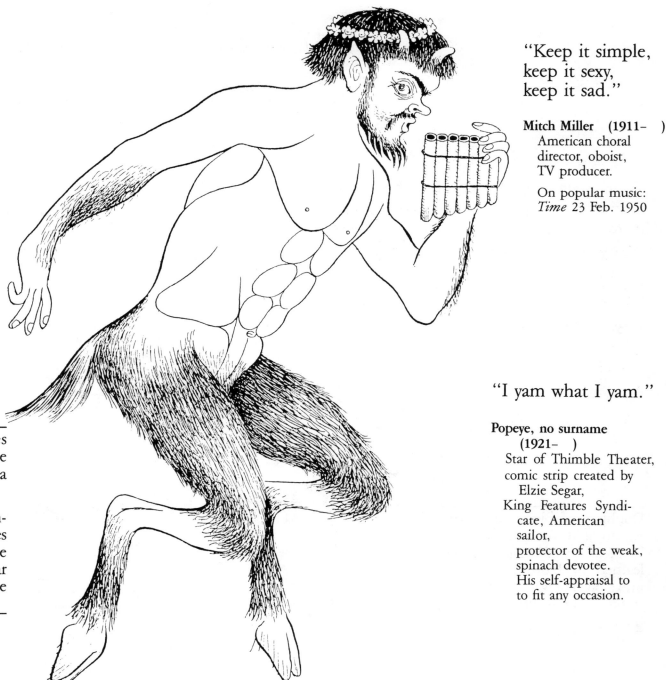

"My men, like satyrs
 grazing on the lawns,
Shall with their goat feet
 dance an antic hay."

Christopher Marlowe **(1564–1593)**
 English poet, dramatist
 blank verse innovator.

 Edward II, I.i. 1592

 hay = country dance
 origin: late 15th c.

Pitch pipes are vertical flutes
bound together raftlike, each one
with a different pitch. Origin, circa
1100 B.C., Far East.

The ancient Greeks called this instrument a *syrinx*, which comes
from a Semitic word meaning "he
hissed" or "whistled." Its popular
name became panpipes, after the
god of nature and lustful love.

"Keep it simple,
keep it sexy,
keep it sad."

Mitch Miller **(1911–   )**
 American choral
 director, oboist,
 TV producer.

 On popular music:
 Time 23 Feb. 1950

"I yam what I yam."

Popeye, no surname
 (1921–   )
 Star of Thimble Theater,
 comic strip created by
  Elzie Segar,
 King Features Syndi-
  cate, American
  sailor,
 protector of the weak,
 spinach devotee.
 His self-appraisal to
 to fit any occasion.

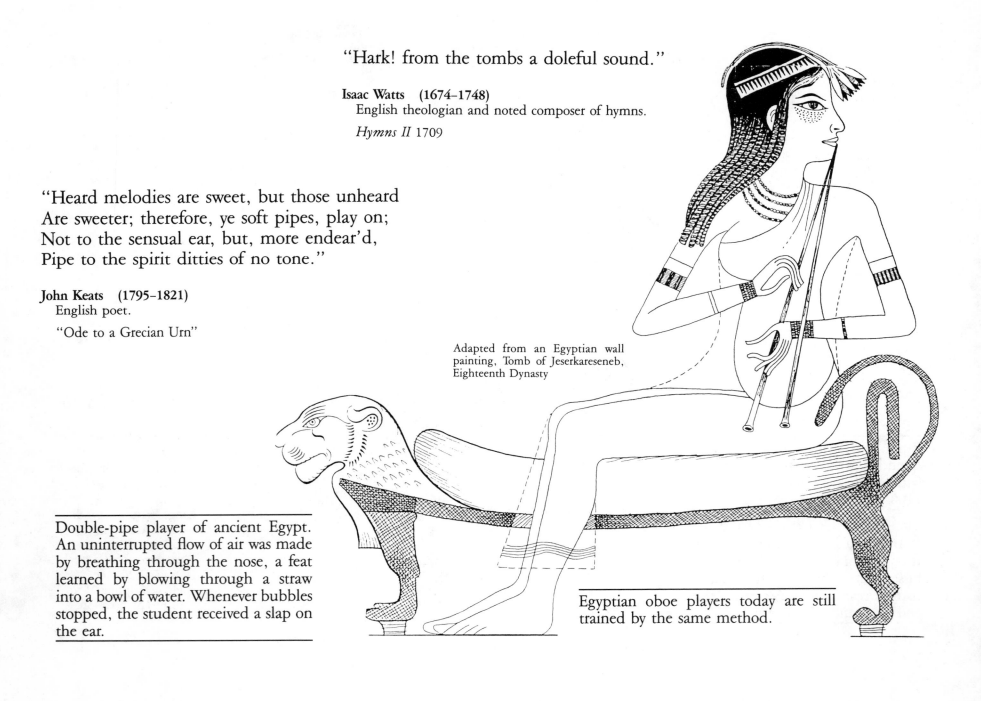

"Hark! from the tombs a doleful sound."

Isaac Watts   (1674–1748)
English theologian and noted composer of hymns.

Hymns II 1709

"Heard melodies are sweet, but those unheard
Are sweeter; therefore, ye soft pipes, play on;
Not to the sensual ear, but, more endear'd,
Pipe to the spirit ditties of no tone."

John Keats   (1795–1821)
English poet.

"Ode to a Grecian Urn"

Adapted from an Egyptian wall painting, Tomb of Jeserkareseneb, Eighteenth Dynasty

Double-pipe player of ancient Egypt. An uninterrupted flow of air was made by breathing through the nose, a feat learned by blowing through a straw into a bowl of water. Whenever bubbles stopped, the student received a slap on the ear.

Egyptian oboe players today are still trained by the same method.

"The sound of the flute will cure epilepsy and a sciatic gout."

Theophrastus (ca. 370–280 B.C.)
Greek philosopher, successor to Aristotle.

"Alcibiades refused to learn the flute, saying that to play on the lute or harp does not in any way disfigure a man's body or face, but one is hardly to be known by the most intimate friends when playing the flute."

Plutarch (ca. 46–120 A.D.)
Greek essayist, biographer.

Lives

Greek *aulos*, played by blowing through a hole in leather headband, the *phorbeia*, which puts pressure on the cheeks' inflation causing them to act as strong bellows.

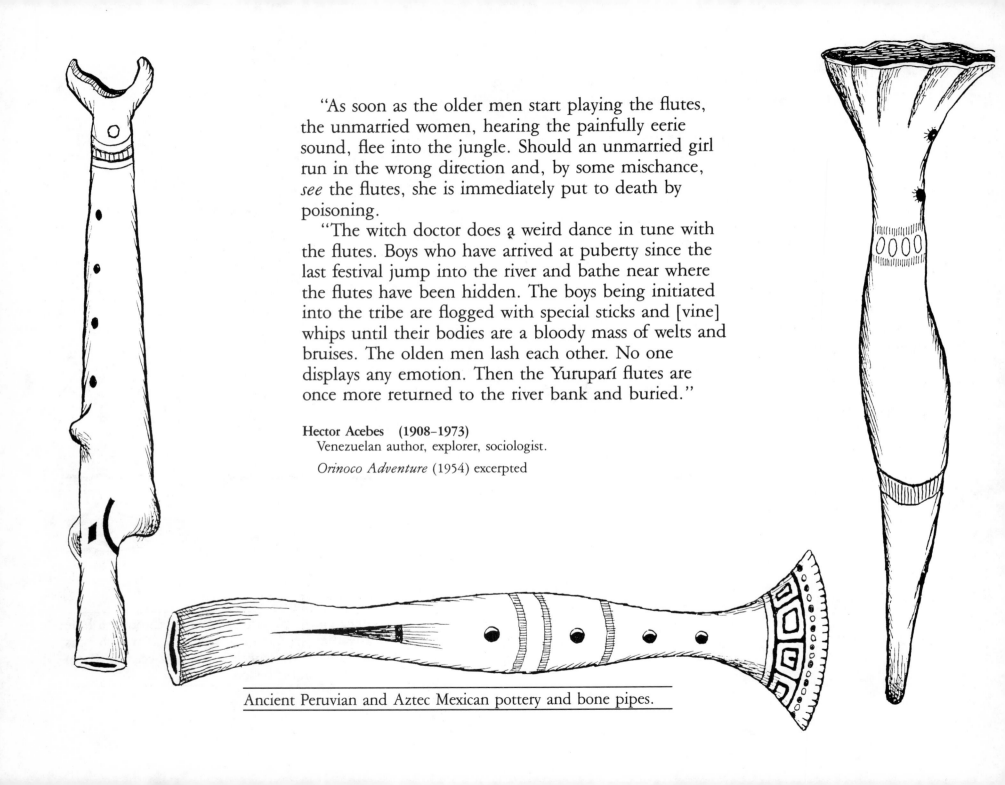

"As soon as the older men start playing the flutes, the unmarried women, hearing the painfully eerie sound, flee into the jungle. Should an unmarried girl run in the wrong direction and, by some mischance, *see* the flutes, she is immediately put to death by poisoning.

"The witch doctor does a weird dance in tune with the flutes. Boys who have arrived at puberty since the last festival jump into the river and bathe near where the flutes have been hidden. The boys being initiated into the tribe are flogged with special sticks and [vine] whips until their bodies are a bloody mass of welts and bruises. The olden men lash each other. No one displays any emotion. Then the Yuruparí flutes are once more returned to the river bank and buried."

Hector Acebes   (1908–1973)
  Venezuelan author, explorer, sociologist.

  Orinoco Adventure (1954) excerpted

Ancient Peruvian and Aztec Mexican pottery and bone pipes.

"These songs are: Indian outside, European inside — Spanish tears in native eyes. All are *mestizo*: Spanish melody and Indian melancholy, when not simply an Indian voice, songs with an intonation peculiar to the region. Take the fragments of an ancestral melody diluted in a Spanish song, played on a primitive instrument, sung by an Indian voice, crude and plaintive, and you have an Indian song."

Andres Henestrosa
  Zapotec writer.

  Mexico South, 1947, Miguel Covarrubias

Primitive
panpipes
in the Andes
of Peru

"The moving accident is not my trade:
To freeze the blood I have no ready arts:
't is my delight, alone in summer shade,
To pipe a simple song for thinking hearts."

William Wordsworth   (1770–1850)
  English poet.

"Raphael de Gangoteña came galloping back to me and wondered where I had been, and he said that we would be at the *Hacienda El Triunfo* in half an hour. He warned that ahead was a deep ravine bridged by two trees with earth stuffed in between, and said not to worry, the horse knew the bridge and would walk across it and just to let him go.

"The bridge came, and after it the *hacienda*. We were met by Don Antonio, the oldest son of the owner.

"What music there can be in the sound of bathwater running into a tub, in hearing a cocktail being mixed; and what pleasure in a simple table laid, and a bottle of wine in a bucket. There was even a bathtowel, a clean one, and a cake of soap."

Ludwig Bemelmans (1898–1962)
   American humorist, artist, author.

The Donkey Inside 1947

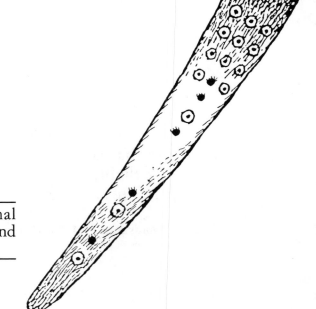

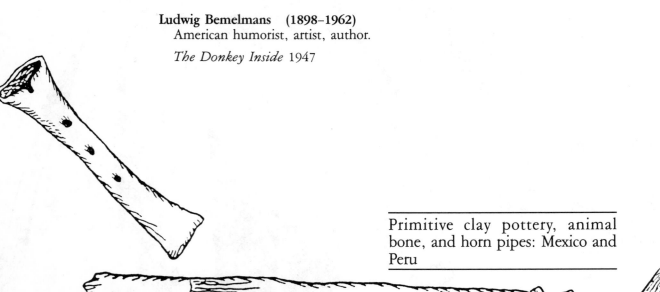

Primitive clay pottery, animal bone, and horn pipes: Mexico and Peru

From Miguel Covarrubias, *Mexico South* 1947

"The way was long, the wind was cold,
The minstrel was infirm and old:
His withered cheek, and tresses gray,
Seem'd to have known a better day."

Sir Walter Scott, Baronet (1771–1832)
Scottish poet and novelist.

The Lay of the Last Minstrel 1830

"I am thy flute;
reveal to me thy will;
breathe into me thy breath
as into a flute . . ."

Prayer of an Inca ruler
ascending his throne.

Street musicians, Tehuantepec, Mexico, performing on the *caja*, a small drum made of a hollowed tree trunk, and the *pito*, a shrill whistle flute made of bamboo. Its ancestor was the ancient *huilacapitztli*, blown by human victims as they climbed the temple steps to the sacrificial altar, or by similarly doomed men as they followed the hearse of a Mayan prince.

"People, if you hear me hummin' on this song
both night and day—
I'm just a poor boy in trouble, trying
to drive my blues away."

Walter Davis, American pianist and folk-singer: "Worried Man Blues"

"Every troublesome and laborious occupation useth musick for solace and recreation; hence it is that manual labourers and mechanical artificers of all sorts keepe such a chaunting in their shoppes — the tailor on his bulk, the shoemaker at his last, the mason at his wall, the ship boy at his oar, and the tinker at his pan."

Thomas Mace (ca. 1620–1710)
English writer on music.

Musick's Monument 1676

"And the music lifted up the listening spirit until it walked, exempt from mortal care, Godlike, o'er the clear billows of sweet sound."

Percy Bysshe Shelley (1792–1822)
English poet.

Prometheus Bound 1819

"They danced gravely in Indian file, to the sound of twenty-three earthen or wooden trumpets of unequal length (about two to four feet long) which can each make only a single note."

André Paul Guillaume Gide (1869–1951)
French novelist, essayist, antiintellectualist.

Travels in the Congo

Gide reports a Dakpas circumcision dance in the Congo, Africa. This drawing however depicts Haitian work chanters with iron-strip clankers and bamboo vaccine pipes setting the pace for a crew of stevedores loading coffee at Cap Haitien, Haiti.

"On these occasions the *vaccine*, a hollow bamboo stalk from two to five feet in length, predominates. *Vaccines* are sometimes gaily painted, and their single low note, blending well with the flat Pétro-type *tambour* also used on such occasions, reverberates through the hills like the cry of some prehistoric owl."

Seldon Rodman (1913–)
American anthologist, poet.

re: Haitian *bambouche*
the social dance

Renaissance in Haiti 1948

"Haitian *danses Congos* are sexual dances . . . no dancing in couples, no waists encircled, no interlacing. It is somewhat like Oriental dancing. All phases of the sexual act, including orgasm, are reproduced. Travelers often imagine they are witnessing Voodoo dances, but the *Congo* is simply a wild frolic."

W.B. Seabrook
American author.

The Magic Island 1929

Une vendeuse de pain and *un conciergerie du hôtel* happily rehashing events of the last evening's *bambouche*: "Whom did what to who, why for, when and where at?"

Homemade feed sack dress
by Singer sewing machine

"In order to compose, all you need do is remember a tune that no one else has thought of."

Robert Alexander Schumann   **(1810–1856)**
German Romantic composer.

"The soft complaining flute
In dying notes, discovers
The woes of hopeless lovers."

John Dryden   **(1631–1700)**
English poet, drama critic.

A Song for St. Cecilia's Day 1687

American Sioux Indian secretly wooing his selected sweetheart with his love flute

"When the young men serenaded, only the flute was forbidden. Why, I asked. Because it was bad for the girls to hear the flute at night."

Ernest Miller Hemingway   **(1899–1961)**
American novelist, short-story writer.

A Farewell to Arms 1929

"... why do so many of us try to explain the beauty of music, thus apparently depriving it of its mystery?"

Leonard Bernstein **(1918–   )**
    American composer, pianist, conductor.

The Unanswered Question 1976

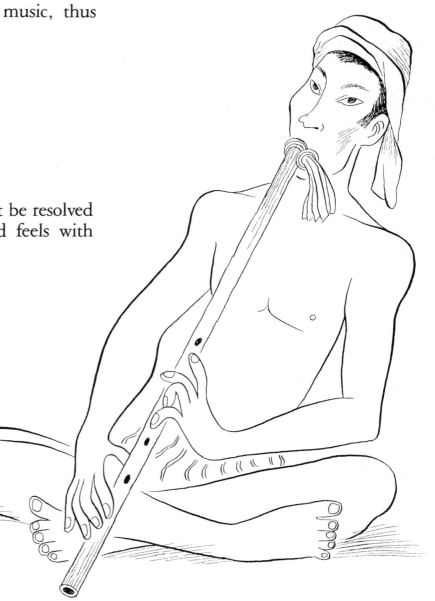

"Music is indivisible. The dualism of feeling and thinking must be resolved to a state of unity in which one thinks with the heart and feels with the brain."

George Szell **(1897–1970)**
    American conductor, pianist, and composer.

Time magazine, 22 February 1963

"I don't want anyone
to admire my pants
in a museum."

Frédéric François Chopin **(1810–1849)**
    Polish composer, pianist
    born Zelazowa–Wola near Warsaw.

Bamboo flute with peacock feathers
Hyderabad, India

New broome swepth cleene."

John Heywood   (1497–1587)
English dramatist, court musician and singer.

Proverbs 1546

"It is the hour when from the boughs
The nightingale's high note is heard
It is the hour when lovers' vows
Seem sweet in every whispered word;
And gentle winds and waters near,
Make music to the lonely ear."

Lord Byron (George Gordon Noel)   (1788–1824)
English poet.

Parisina I.

"Loneliness . . . is and always has been
the central and inevitable experience
of every man."

Thomas Clayton Wolfe   (1900–1938)
American author, celebrated for his epic trilogy
of Southern family life.

You Can't Go Home Again 1937

". . . Superimposed on Buddhist Thai culture is a rash of comic books, an erratic effort at television, and battalions of American trained teachers, nurses, agronomists, and architects. The American orange pop called Green Spot is shipped from the United States in the form of syrup, bottled in a gleaming picture-window plant in Bangkok, and celebrated over the local radio with a singing commercial . . . Thai words set to the song, 'I Whistle a Happy Tune' . . . from the musical comedy, *The King and I*, a Broadway-Hollywood version of 'Anna and the King of Siam.' "

Oden Meeker **(1919–1976)**
American author, travel journalist.

The Little World of Laos 1959

"... The movement was of the slow undulating *danse du ventre*, and was not done, unlike our own Western imitations of this dance, as a sexless contortion achieved by an acrobatic dancer on a carrot diet. The woman moved in a slow feline animal grace, her head lolling indolently, her eyes almost closed, manifestly in the assurance that her undulations would excite the masculine members of her audience, and thus her movement became more and more relaxed."

Angna Enters
American dancer, celebrated mime .
Note from travel journal, 1933, "Morocco."
From *First Person Plural* 1937.

"Her feet beneath her petticoat,
Like little mice, stole in and out,
As if they feared the light;
But, oh, she dances in such a way!
No sun upon an Easter-day
Is half so fine a sight."

Sir John Suckling   (1609–1642)
English poet, playwright. Inherited fortune,
age 18. Playboy gallant, gambler, court of Charles I.
A suicide, by poison, age 33, in fear of poverty.

"O body swayed to music,
  O brightening glance,
How can we know the dancer
  from the dance?"

William Butler Yeats (1865–1939)
  Irish poet, essayist.

Among School Children

"When a beauteous
Nymph decays
We say, she's
past her Dancing Days."

Jonathan Swift (1667–1745)
  British satirist, Dean of St. Patrick's, Dublin.

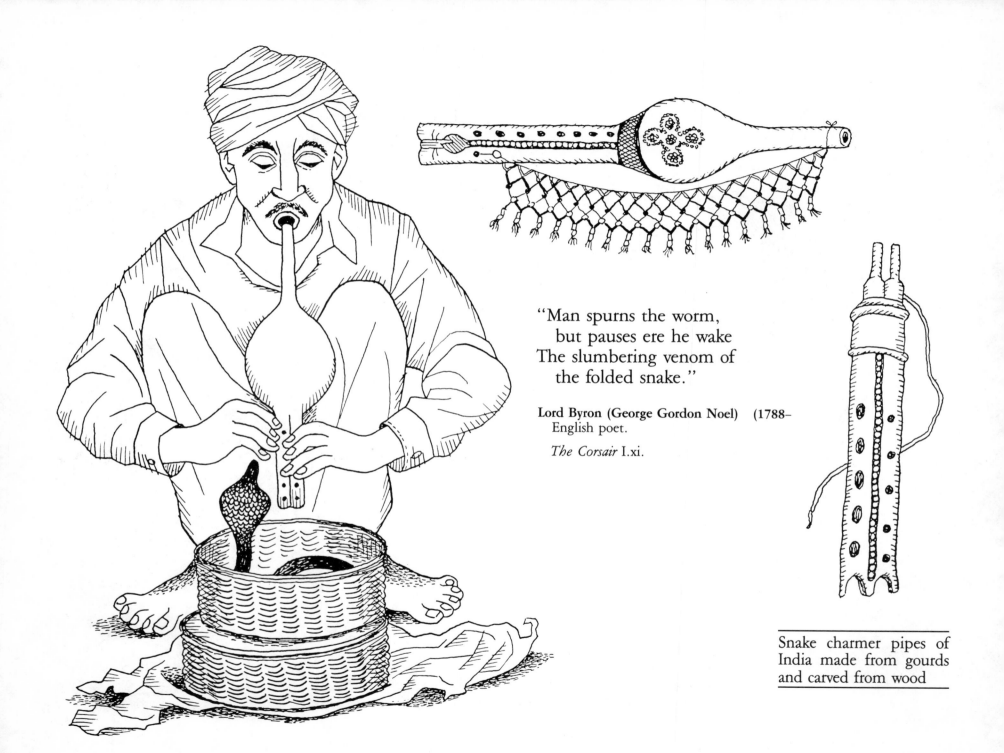

"Man spurns the worm,
    but pauses ere he wake
The slumbering venom of
    the folded snake."

Lord Byron (George Gordon Noel)   (1788–
English poet.

The Corsair I.xi.

Snake charmer pipes of
India made from gourds
and carved from wood

Early one morning Datta, the guide furnished by the government, came by my hotel to say that the pass into Srinigar, Kashmir, was still closed for flying, so this day we visit snake charmers at Muralband, a Delhi suburb where many of them live. Only a few were at home. Most were in the city charming the tourists. In one hut an old man brought out a basket full of small cobras and dumped them on the earthen floor. A kid, about four, stepped barefoot amidst the mass of wriggling snakes, gingerly picked up one and carried it to the charmer who sat cross-legged on a mat against one wall, blowing on his decorated gourd pipe. The cobra didn't show much interest, just kept bobbing up and down, its neck inflated into an ominous hood by the reptile pushing its long anterior ribs up and forward. It's the sign that a cobra is annoyed — not a reassuring sight to someone who was brought up on Adam and Eve. Cobras are highly poisonous and each year kill thousands of India's citizens, who grant the sinister reptile holy-being status. A gone-away Presbyterian *might* be immune to attack. I hoped. Well, after interminable piping and hypnotic swaying with no visible enthusiasm from the snake, the charmer gave up, explaining to Datta that these cobras were just breaking into the act, needed a lot more training. We backed out of the hut — *very* carefully. I wanted to hiss, "Amateur," at the cobra but was too scared. Besides, I figured it probably didn't dig English. — *B.B.*

Designs from a rock-cut panel in a temple at Mahabalipuram, Madras, southern India.

Adapted from a
Japanese print

"The flute is not
an instrument with
a good moral effect.
It is too exciting."

Aristotle (**384–322** B.C.)
Ancient Greek philosopher.

Politics, a treatise of
the period, 347–335 B.C.

"Zeal's a dreadful
termagant, that
teaches saints
to tear and rant."

Samuel Butler (**1612–1680**)
English author, poet.

Hudibras 1612–1680

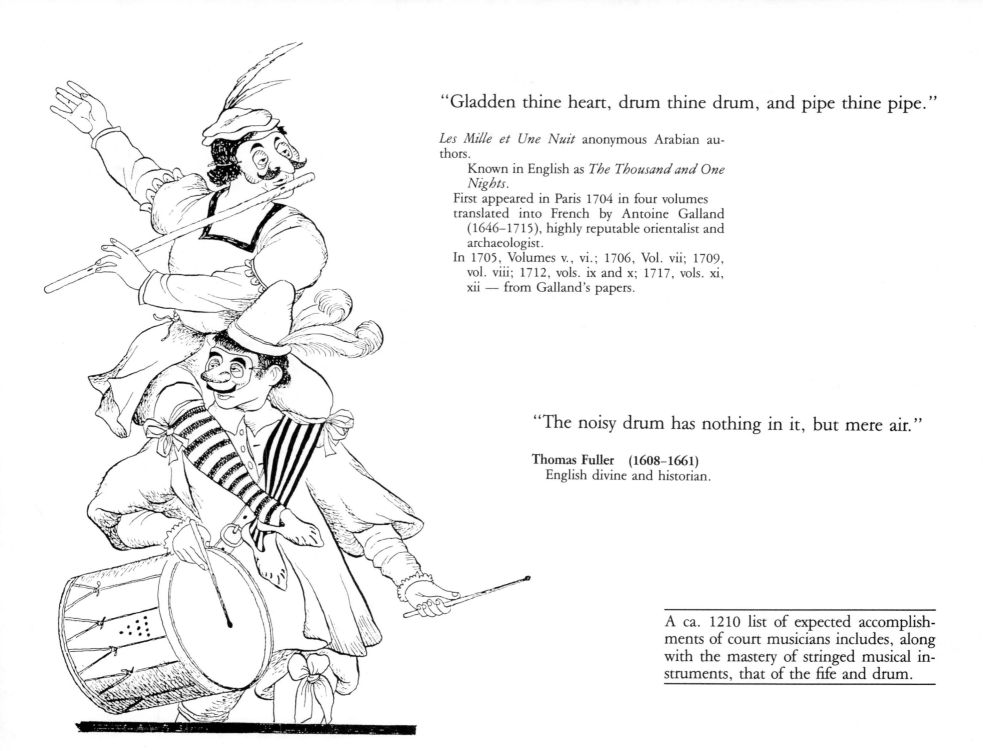

"Gladden thine heart, drum thine drum, and pipe thine pipe."

Les Mille et Une Nuit anonymous Arabian authors.
   Known in English as *The Thousand and One Nights*.
First appeared in Paris 1704 in four volumes translated into French by Antoine Galland (1646–1715), highly reputable orientalist and archaeologist.
In 1705, Volumes v., vi.; 1706, Vol. vii; 1709, vol. viii; 1712, vols. ix and x; 1717, vols. xi, xii — from Galland's papers.

"The noisy drum has nothing in it, but mere air."

Thomas Fuller   (1608–1661)
   English divine and historian.

A ca. 1210 list of expected accomplishments of court musicians includes, along with the mastery of stringed musical instruments, that of the fife and drum.

Adapted from an acrylic painting by I Watan Turun
Bidari-Bidari Collection of Koes Studio, Bali

"They have no written music. They learned by ear . . . no one ever forgets or makes a mistake . . . they break into strange incredible syncopations; they flutter rhythms as blithe as Mozart's."

Hickman Powell
American author.

The Last Paradise

The quote refers to the gamelin orchestras of Bali.

"All my concerts had no sounds in them: they were completely silent . . . people had to make their own music in their minds."

Yoko Ono   (1933–   )
Rock concert and album producer, widow of Beatles' John Lennon.

Interview: Johnathon Cott, *Rolling Stone* 1968

"Why, a spirit is such a little thing, that I have
heard a man, who was a great scholar, say that he'll
dance ye a hornpipe upon the point of a needle."

Joseph Addison (1672–1719)
  English essayist, poet and man of letters.

  The Drummer, I.i 1716

"Sweet sounds, oh, beautiful music, do not cease!
Reject me not into the world again.
With you alone is excellence and peace,
Mankind made plausible, his purpose plain."

Edna St. Vincent Millay (1892–1950)
  American poet (Mrs. Eugen Jan Boissevain).
  Pulitzer prize (1923), playwright, opera librettist.

  "On Hearing a Symphony of Beethoven"

"If you are happy you can always learn to dance."

Santha Rama Rau (1923–1950)
  Balinese folk saying:

  Santha Rama Rau, *East of Home*, 1950

19th century
Neapolitan
dancers

"On with the dance! let joy be unconfined;
No sleep till morn, when Youth and Pleasure meet
To chase the glowing Hours with flying feet."

Lord Byron (George Gordon Noel)   (1788–1824)
English poet, his family's 6th Baron, lame from birth.

Childe Harold 1809. The quote describes his coming-of-age party.

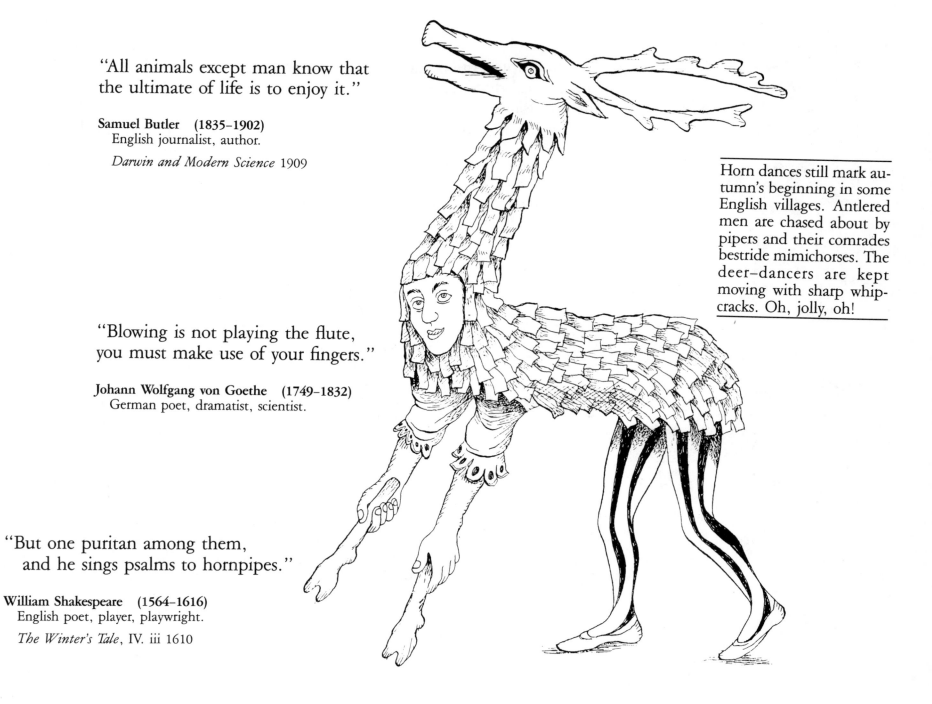

"All animals except man know that the ultimate of life is to enjoy it."

Samuel Butler (1835–1902)
English journalist, author.

Darwin and Modern Science 1909

Horn dances still mark autumn's beginning in some English villages. Antlered men are chased about by pipers and their comrades bestride mimichorses. The deer–dancers are kept moving with sharp whip-cracks. Oh, jolly, oh!

"Blowing is not playing the flute, you must make use of your fingers."

Johann Wolfgang von Goethe (1749–1832)
German poet, dramatist, scientist.

"But one puritan among them, and he sings psalms to hornpipes."

William Shakespeare (1564–1616)
English poet, player, playwright.

The Winter's Tale, IV. iii 1610

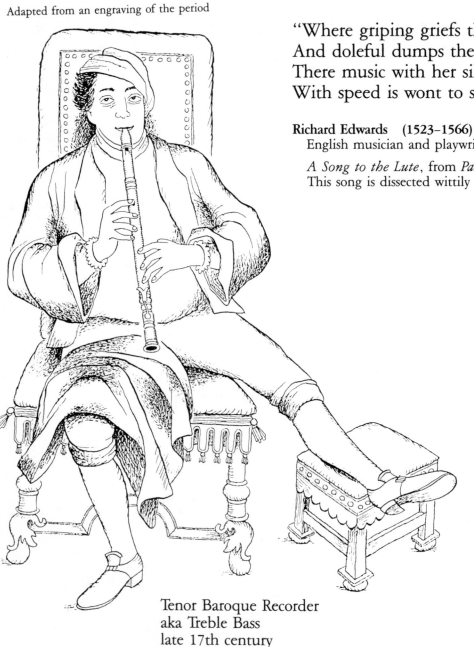

Adapted from an engraving of the period

Tenor Baroque Recorder
aka Treble Bass
late 17th century

"Where griping griefs the heart would wound
And doleful dumps the mind oppress,
There music with her silver sound
With speed is wont to send redress."

Richard Edwards   (1523–1566)
English musician and playwright.

A Song to the Lute, from *Paradise of Dainty Devices* 1575
This song is dissected wittily in *Romeo and Juliet* IV, v. 127 fol.

"He knew music was good,
but it didn't sound right."

George Ade   (1866–1944)
American humorist, journalist, author.

*Fable of the Married Girl Who Ran
the Eating Station for the Luminaries*
George was inclined to verbosity in story titles.

The earliest clue to the name of the musical instrument called the recorder appears in the household accounts for the year 1388 of the Earl of Derby, later Henry IV. An entry notes the gift, evidently from some Italian nobleman, of: *la fistula nomine Ricordo* — "a flute called a keepsake."

"The shrill hornpipe
sounds to bacchanals."

John Dryden (1631–1700)
English poet.
Aeneid translation

"Sailors get money like horses
and spend it like asses."

Tobias George Smollett (1721–1771)
Scottish satirist, novelist,
surgeon of the Royal Navy.
Explaining an old folk saying
about seafarers in

The Adventures of Peregrine Pickle 1751

The hornpipe is an English folk dance of the
16th century, so named for the pipe that
accompanies it, fashioned with bell and
mouthpiece of animal horn. The dance has
been widely adopted by sailors who perform
it with folded arms and a host of lewd ges-
tures and movements.

HENRY
the Eighth

Adapted from
Holbein portrait
1537

Musical instruments of Henry VIII at West-minster Palace, England, 1542: 65 flutes, 59 recorders, 25 lutes, 22 clarinets, 20 regals (portable organs), 15 shawms (French oboes, *chalemels*), 14 virginals, 11 viols, seven glitterns, two clavichords, one bag-pipe, and what must have been one barrel organ or a hurdy–gurdy . . . "oone instru-ment what goith with a whele and withoute playeing upon, of woode vernisshed yellowe and painted blewe with six rounde plates of silver pounced with antique worke garnished with an edge of copper and gilt . . ."

"So is music an asylum.
It takes us out of the actual
and whispers to us dim secrets
that startle our wonder as to
who we are, and for what,
whence and whereto."

Ralph Waldo Emerson   **(1803–1882)**
    American poet, essayist
    Journals 1836–38

Henry decided that the yard mea-sure would be the distance from the tip of his nose to the length of a bass recorder.

"From thense the whole court removed to Windsor, there beginning his progress and exercising himself dailie in shooting, singing, dansing, wrestling, casting of the barre, plaieing at the recorders, flute, virginals, in setting of songs, and making of ballads."

Raphael Holinshed (ca. 1527–1580)
English chronicler, from a 1510 report of one of the king's investigative tours around his realm.

"*Item:*

a Case couered with crimeson vellat hauinge locke and all other garnishments to the same of Siluer gilte with VIII recorders of Iuerie in the same Case the two bases garnished with Siluer and guilte."

One of thirteen items listing the seventy-six recorders, of all sizes ("great base to smale") belonging to King Henry VIII of England and Ireland from 1509 to 1547, a reign of 38 years.

Henry Tudor (1491–1547)
Third child and second son of Henry VII and Elizabeth of York. Accomplished scholar, linguist, musician, and athlete. Married six times. His passion for music did not prevent him from chopping off the heads of two of his mates: Anne Boleyn, No.2, and Catherine Howard, No. 5; nor from divorcing No.1, Catherine of Aragon (his brother's widow), and No. 4, Anne of Cleves. (No. 3, Jane Seymour had a natural death; No. 6, Catherine Parr, survived him.)

translations:
coured = covered / *crimeson* = crimson / *hauinge* = having
Siluer = silver / *Iuerie* = Ivory / *guilte* = gilt

Henry's costume: red velvet lined with sable, embroidered in gold. Elaborate codpiece, White hose with garter: '*Honi soit qui mal i pense.*' White shoes, slashed. Black bonnet, white plume, underside sewn with gold tags.

"Spare your breath to cool your pottage."

Miguel de Cervantes y Saavedra   (1547–1616)
  Spanish poet, dramatist, novelist, social critic.

  Don Quixote II.v.

"Has a woman who knew
that she was well-dressed
ever caught a cold?"

Friedrich Wilhelm Nietzsche   (1844–1900)
  German philosopher.

  The Twilight of the Idols 1889

"There is something
in the wind."

William Shakespeare   (1564–1616)
  English poet, player, playwright.

  The Comedy of Errors 1594

After 16th century engraving by Tobias Stimmer

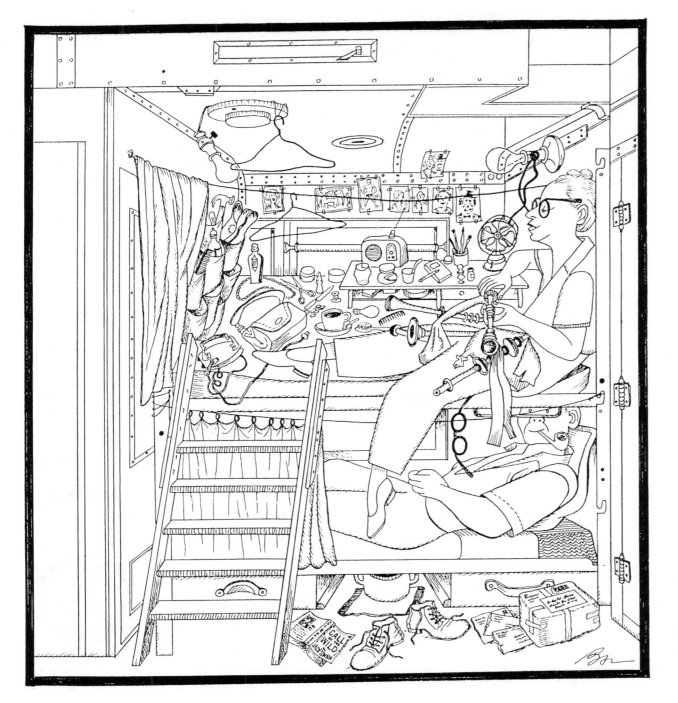

"Some men there are
    love not a gaping pig;
Some that are mad
    if they behold a cat;
And others, when
    the bag-pipe
    sings i' the nose,
Cannot contain
    their urine."

William Shakespeare   (1564–1616)
The Merchant of Venice IV.i.

Bagpipes are from long ago. The Greeks knew them. Romans aroused their soldiers with bagpipes. Historians reveal that Nero played ". . . the pipe with his mouth, and bag thrust under his arm." Bagpipes are best-loved by Scots, Welsh, and Irish. In India they are *poobgi*; *biniou*, Brittany; *cornemuse*, France; *Dudelsack*, or *Sackpfeife*, Germany.

Meet Lulu Adams, English musical clown, repairing her comedy bagpipes on the Ringling Bros. Circus train, season of 1948

LULU, ROSE, & The Bagpipes

In 1948 The Greatest Show On Earth contracted a married couple of musical clowns from England, Gilbert and Lulu Adams, whose act had impressed the big show's president, Johnny North, during his annual talent search overseas.

In late afternoon of the day before the circus's opening at the old Madison Square Garden in New York City, Lulu's husband, while doing a circus-promotion broadcast on local radio, suffered a heart attack and dropped dead.

North didn't press Lulu to honor her contract, but being a proper British lady, she did, appearing as a single pantomime–Pierrette, with curly silverblonde wig, playing her squealing bagpipes. She worked uncomplaining through the long, dreary Manhattan engagement, then went on the road, bravely alone, on the show's transcontinental tour to more than 100 cities, traveling about 22,000 railroad miles. She became friends with the circus's only other woman clown, Rose Hanlon, working wife of Bill, elder brother of Fred, British clowns whose uncles were the fantastic Hanlon–Lees troupe of knockabout clowning, staged with elaborate scenic trickery, never since duplicated.

In '48 Rose's specialty was a comedy solo on a trombone, the slide of which was rigged with wires to her roomy trouser legs so that they were pulled up and down as the horn's shaft slid

forth and back on the horn. Simple, but always good for a chuckle.

Rose was near-sighted and often by mistake she sat on Lulu's bagpipes as they lay on her canvas chair in the big top's backyard, in the area nearest the tent's back entrance door, a favorite lounge spot for performers. There, during performances, while waiting their turns, they sunned, read books, did needlework, gossiped and warmed up.

Rose always blamed Lulu for leaving her bagpipes for someone to sit on by mistake. True, all the circus folding chairs looked alike but true also, each had its owner's name boldly painted on the canvas or the sticks.

Rose seldom was logical. She'd once suffered a terrible automobile accident that gave her a badly fractured skull and required much internal surgery. Sometimes she'd sit by mistake on the bagpipes when they were on Lulu's trunk in the LDR, ladies–dressing–room, half of the wardrobe tent where all performers dressed — except the stars, who had their own little square tents pitched in the backyard.

Whenever the bagpipes were damaged on the trunk top, Rose renounced blame, stating that she couldn't possibly be guilty because no circus trouper ever sat on another trouper's trunk—that was the code.

Rose didn't always play with a full deck, but Lulu was kind to her and never fussed over the interminable repairs. She and Rose remained friends, though Lulu pretty much was a loner. She minded her own business by day and repaired her bagpipes by night.

Lulu didn't often meander within the confines of her sleeping car, except sometimes after the evening show she'd venture to our sleeper's deadend, bucked up against the train's caboose. There our genial porter, Smiley, operated a tiny kitchen which offered such fare as mulligan stew, chops, hamburgers, and a steak if ordered in advance. His fridge was well–stocked with beer — no license — and he poured hard stuff from bottles stashed under the counter that blocked his doorway.

Lulu, Rose and I met often at this spa. On some nights, we'd coax Rose into warbling the oldtimey British music-hall songs from her wind-pudding days in honky-tonk revues and on the vaudeville circuits of the provinces. One that I well remember, every inflection:

"Ah don' wanna go to *Mex*-i-co,
"All ah want is some good ol' *dough*,
When ah get that *in* my hand,
You can have your *one*-night-stand,
You won't see me around here *ah*-gain,
Ah'm gonna get me on to a *train*,
Did somebody mention *Enn*-Wy-See?
That's Home-sweet-*home* to Me-e-eee!"

"Sing it again, Rose . . ."

"Smiley, I'm springin' for another round. Fill 'em up."

Says Rose, "Make mine a boiler-maker."

And we'd get it again, plus a couple of other vintage beloveds, and the rails would be clickety-clacking as the circus train plunged through the dead of night, past clanging crossing-bells and blurred trackside houses with doused lights, thru little towns with only their street lamps still on.

"I can't never sleep with all that noise," says Rose. "I'll never get used to it — unless maybe I have a few belts."

"To me," says Smiley, "it's a lullaby."

"That's 'cause you ain't over the wheels, an' you're not in no upper — my Bill's glommed onto the lower."

Ah, those thousand–and–one nights on the circus train. Sing it again, Rose — with feeling. Set 'em up again, Smiley. Tomorrow's another day.

I quote Jim Tully's *Circus Parade*:

> "The Moss-haired Girl, the Strong Woman, Aimee the Beautiful Fat Girl, the Lion Tamer, Whiteface, Lefita, and Jock are people I shall never meet again. But I would trade the empty honor of a writer's name to be once again their comrade."

What the Clowns Play

Best way for clowns to get attention in the hurly-burly circus is to make noise, so they favor music makers that are loud and lend themselves to comedy: brasses, the brassier the better; drums and cymbals (often, just crashing pie tins); whistles, clarinet, saxophone occasionally; strings rarely, tiny fiddle or gimmicked bass viol.

Grock had lots of fun with a grand piano, but he didn't have to tour with it.

Theobald Boehm (1794–1881)

The most bitter feud in all flutedom began in 1831 between Theobald Boehm, principal flutist to the King of Bavaria, and William Gordon, a former captain in the Swiss Guards of French king Charles X. While building his newly invented flute, Gordon lived nine months in Boehm's Munich household, making use of his host's craftsmen and seeking advice from Boehm. In 1832, Boehm invented a flute with innovations that outshone those of Gordon's new instrument. He was incensed and accused Boehm of stealing his ideas from Gordon. Boehm denied the charges and soon had a factory turning out his own new flutes. The dispute festered for years until finally Gordon went insane and died. Today Boehm is regarded as the creator of the flute as we know it. No major changes have been made to date, except the important addition of a B-flat lever. — *B.B.*

Early flute of Theobald Boehm.

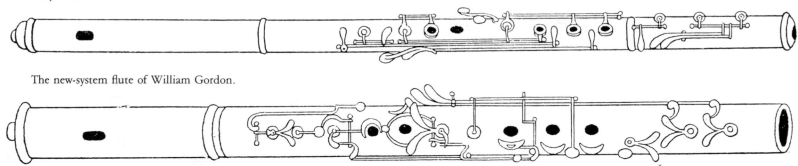

The new-system flute of William Gordon.

Comparison of the controversial Boehm and Gordon flute systems.

A tutor who tooted a flute
Tried to teach two young tutors to toot;
Said the two to the tutor:
"Is it harder to toot, or
To tutor two tutors to toot?"

Anonymous
Old English
limerick

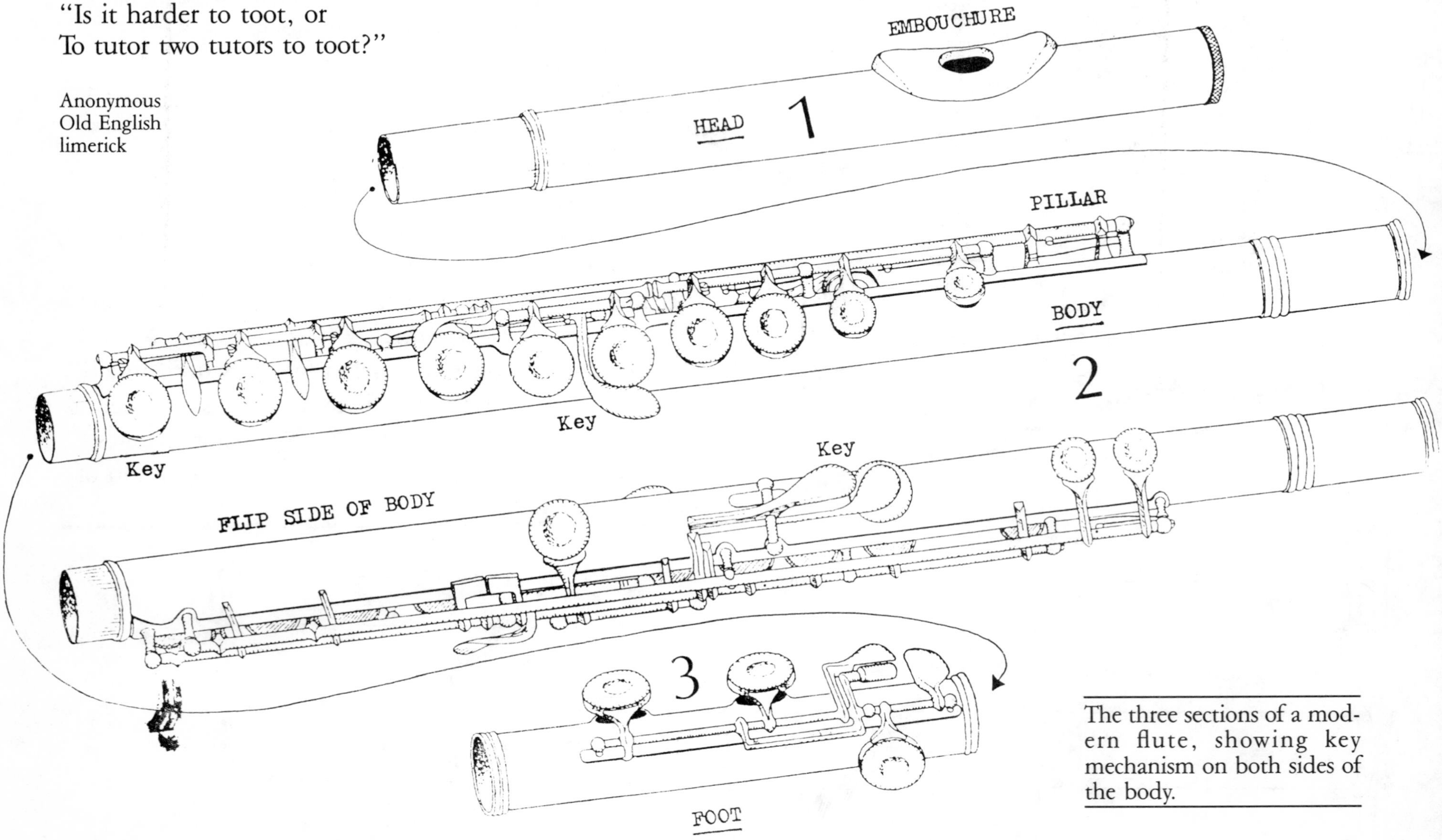

EMBOUCHURE

HEAD 1

PILLAR

BODY

2

Key

Key

Key

Key

FLIP SIDE OF BODY

3

FOOT

The three sections of a modern flute, showing key mechanism on both sides of the body.

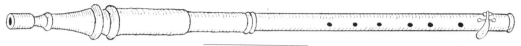
English Flagolet

FLUTE MAKERS

At one time or another flutes have been made of marble and jade (Greeks/Chinese); terra cotta, clay (Portuguese); eagle, vulture bones; animal horn; porcelain, Dresden china; tortoise shell inlaid in gold; *papier maché*; ivory, glass, and even leather — by an Edinburgh shoemaker in 1789. John Bunyan in jail carved a flute from a prison stool leg. Walking stick flutes were popular in 1880. Often two such made a long staff on which to play duets. Flutes also could harbor a sword. Flutes have been made from cocus wood, ebony, laurel, pine, and South American granadilla. Majority of modern flutes are made in Boston, Mass., or Elkhart, Indiana. A flute maker needs patience and iron nerves as measurements must be made to a hair's breadth, and everything fitted exact to a T.

FLUTE DISASTERS

Freak flute catastrophes: During a ballet, New York, 1953, a flutist touched his silver flute to both his lighted music stand and to the metal railing around the orchestra pit. Somehow the contact caused a short circuit. In a blinding flash the flute's keys, springs, and solder became a melted mess. Luckily, the flute player wasn't burned but his instrument had to go in for extensive repairs. Once, during a circus performance, a runaway drill horse kicked a flute and two front teeth from the mouth of a bandsman. A flutist visiting backstage at the Metropolitan Opera accidently dropped his flute into a tub of scenery paint. Every part down to the lowliest screw had to be dismantled and wiped clean. Flutes are lost in fires and floods, and sometimes fall overboard from boats. Even the slightest accident is disaster to a flute. — *B.B.*

Bass Flute 1751

Flutists remain generally unknown outside the profession, but music lovers are aware of many of the better ones. Severino Gazzelloni is considered one of the world's leading flute virtuosos. Jean-Pierre Rampal and James Galway are others of the famous — two of the best. Also well known are Pierre Herichez, Maxence Larrieu, Alain Marion, Claude Monteux, and Michel Bebost — all Frenchmen, traditionally the finest wind instrumentalists. Noteworthy flute players in the United States are Julius Baker, first flutist, New York Philharmonic; Harold Bennett, formerly of the NBC Symphony Orchestra; James Politos, Metropolitan Opera first flutist; and Sebastian Caratelli, Radio City Music Hall Orchestra. Other outstanding male flutists: Marcel Moyse and son Louis; William Heil, Paige Brooks, and John Wummer. Noted women flutists: Elaine Shaffer, Paula Sylvester, Nancy Urrelman, and Doriot Dwyer. Two master flutists of recent past: William Kincaid, of the Philadelphia Orchestra, and Georges Barrère, celebrated first flutist with the New York Symphony Orchestra under Walter Damrosch. Barrère's superlative playing is still held in highest regard.

Pioneer jazz flutist was Waymen Carver, who played with the Chick Webb band, 1937. A West Coast jazz man, Harry Klee, fluted a bit, 1944, but Frank Wellington of Kansas City was the first jazz star to record as flute soloist. Then came Frank Wess, Count Basie band, and Bud Shank in California. Other jazz flute virtuosi of note: Jerome Richardson (also did piccolo); Paul Horn (his mother was Irving Berlin's pianist); Bobby Jasper, a Belgian; Yuseff Lateef (aka William Evans), Dizzy Gillespie band. Most gifted modern flutist in jazz: Jay Solomon (Herbie) Mann. Flutes now often pop up in rock and folk rock. Historic off-beat flute virtuosi: Frenchman, Philbert, on one-note flute, court of Louis XIV; Louis Hotteterre, late 1660s played first transverse flute to appear in Paris Opera; and Johann Joachim Quantz, most distinguished flutist of his time (1697–1773). Taught flute *secretly* to young crown prince of Prussia because his father, the king, had vowed to behead anyone who'd teach his son "such a vile, dreadful, disgusting musical instrument." — *B.B.*

" 'Then someone came to me and said
The little fishes are in bed . . .
I took a corkscrew from the shelf:
I went to wake them up myself.
And when I found the door was locked,
I pulled and pushed and kicked and knocked
And when I found the door was shut,
I tried to turn the handle, but —'

'Is that all:' Alice timidly asked.
'That's all,' said Humpty Dumpty.
'Good-bye.'

Charles Lutwidge Dodgson   (1832–1898) — aka Lewis Carroll

English mathematician
and author, best-known
for the childhood classic
*Alice's Adventures
in Wonderland*, 1865

Charles Tripp
"The Armless Wonder"
(1855–1939)

Eli Bowen
"The Legless Acrobat"
(1844–1927)

2
DAYS
ONLY

OPERA HOUSE NEXT WEEK

Count
REBSOMEN

WORLD
FAMED

ONE-ARM
FLUTIST

Oldtime circus and carnival Side Show stars

Charles to Eli: "Bowen, watch your step!" . . . Eli to Charles: "Keep your hands off me, Tripp!"

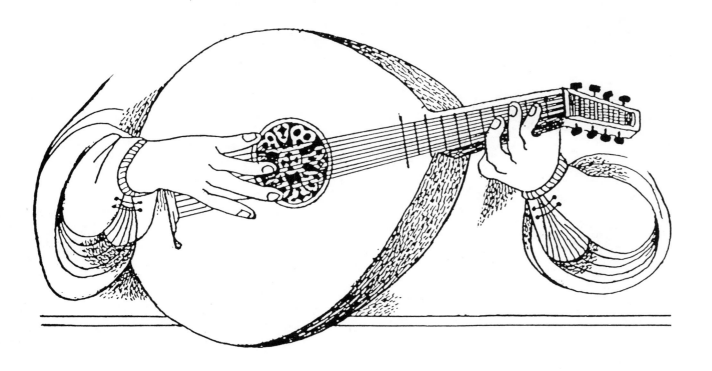

plucking

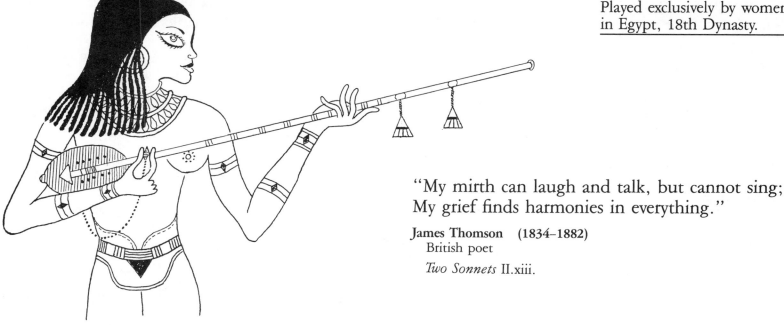

Adapted from Egyptian wall painting
Tomb of Jeserkareseneb, Eighteenth Dynasty

"My mirth can laugh and talk, but cannot sing;
My grief finds harmonies in everything."

James Thomson   **(1834–1882)**
British poet

Two Sonnets II.xiii.

"In the very beginning the first utterings of creation
sounded in the language of waters, in the voice of the wind."

Rabindranath Tagore   **(1861–1941)**
Hindu poet, philosopher, educator.

Lipika

The Egyptian two-string, long, plucked lute dates back to at least 2,000 B.C. It originated in Assyria and its Arabic names is *ud*, which means flexible stick.

"Fate does not jest
and events are not
a matter of chance —
there is no existence
out of nothing."

Gamal Abdel Nasser **(1918–1970)**
Leader of the Arab unification,
second president of Egypt.

Liberation: Philosophy of the Revolution 1955

"Short swallow flights of song, that dip
Their wings in tears, and swim away."

Lord Alfred Tennyson **(1809–1892)**
English Poet Laureate.

In Memoriam XLVIII

"We hanged our harps
upon the willows."

The Holy Bible
King James version
"Psalms" 137:2.

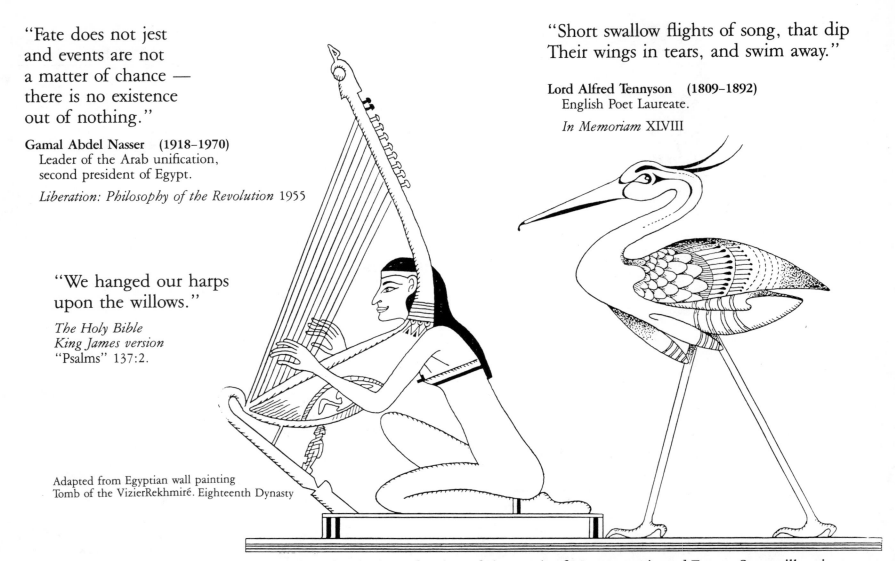

Adapted from Egyptian wall painting
Tomb of the VizierRekhmiré. Eighteenth Dynasty

For 30 centuries the harp dominated the music of Mesopotamia and Egypt. Spun-silk strings were plucked by both queens and commoner virtuosi, who usually were blinded to prevent their viewing of palatial high-jinks.

"Not to know what happened before one was born is to remain a child."

Marcus Tullius Cicero (106–43 B.C.)
Roman orator and politician.

De Oratore, XXXIV

"I heard among the solitary hills
Low breathings coming after me, and sounds
Of undistinguishable motion, steps
Almost as silent as the turf they trod.

William Wordsworth
English poet.

The Prelude, I

"Talking is like playing on the harp; there is as much in laying the hands on the strings to stop their vibration as in twanging them to bring out their music."

Oliver Wendell Holmes (1809–1894)
American writer, physician.

The Autocrat of the Breakfast Table 1856

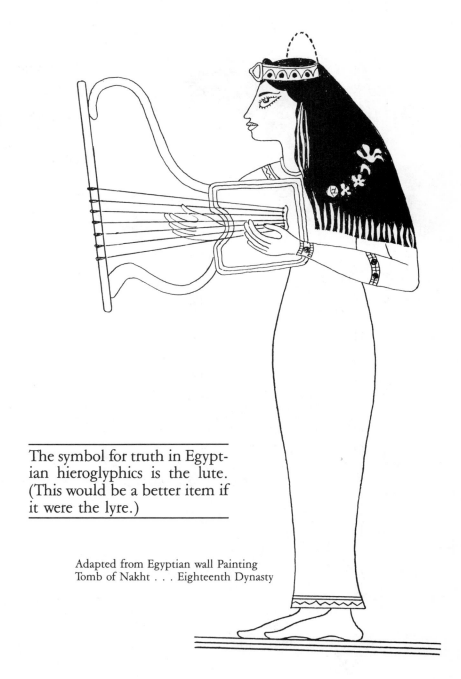

The symbol for truth in Egyptian hieroglyphics is the lute. (This would be a better item if it were the lyre.)

Adapted from Egyptian wall Painting
Tomb of Nakht . . . Eighteenth Dynasty

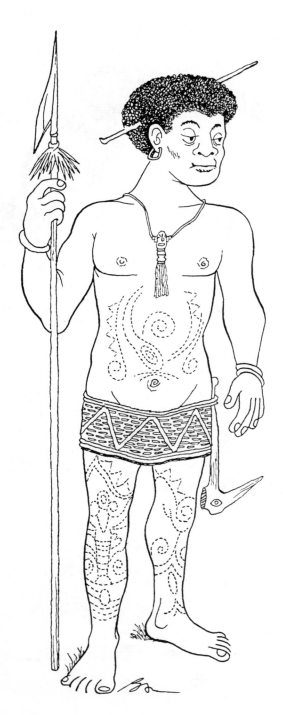

"Music is not a science any more than poetry is.
It is a sublime instinct, like genius of all kinds."

Ouida (Marie Louise de la Ramée) **(1839–1908)**
    English novelist
    Her odd *nom de plume* derived from
    a childish attempt to pronounce her
    given name, Louisa

"Music is the nearest at hand, the most orderly,
the most delicate, and the most perfect,
of all bodily pleasures . ."

John Ruskin **(1819–1900)**
Scottish author, critic, socialist
Music in Greek Education 1869

Primitive music-maker, using a
flat rock for resonance and an
earthen cavity as sound chamber

"I still say
if you got to plug it in
it's not a musical instrument,
it's a machine."

Jake Vest (1954–   )
   Cartoonist (comic panel, *That's Jake*,
   Tribune Media Services, Inc.)

   Orlando Sentinel, Florida 2 May 1985

"Enough of clouds, waves, aquariums, nymphs, and
perfumes of the night. We need a music that is down
to earth — an everyday music."

Jean Cocteau   (1889–1963)
   French poet, dramatist, literary modernist,
   producer of surrealistic films.

"The first man who balanced a straw upon his nose . . .
deserved the applause of mankind, not on account of what
he did, but of the dexterity which he exhibited."

Dr. Samuel Johnson   (1709–1784)
   English writer, lexicographer.

To make music, fingers
pluck the tuned metal
tongues.

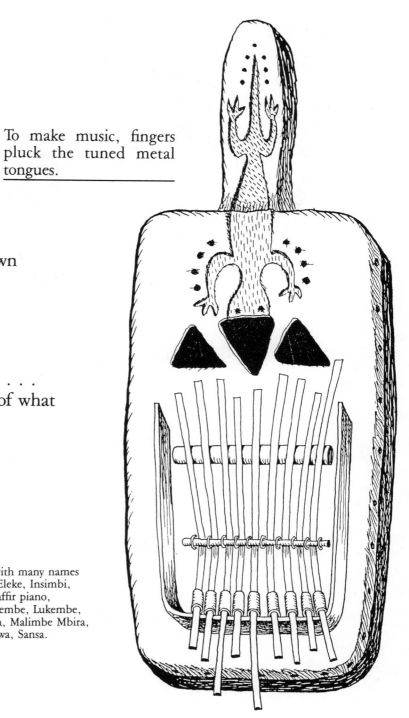

African, with many names
Agidibo, Eleke, Insimbi,
Kasayi, Kaffir piano,
Kisanji, Kembe, Lukembe,
Madujmba, Malimbe Mbira,
Oopoolhawa, Sansa.

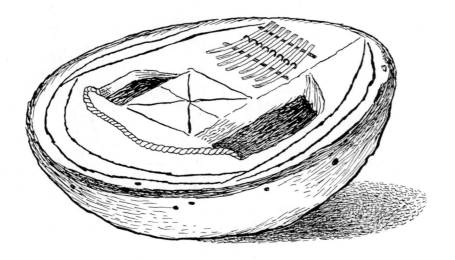

"Music is the art of sounds
in the movement of time."

Ferruccio Benevenuto Busoni (1866–1924)
  Italian pianist, composer.
  The Essence of Music June 1924

"A portable companion always ready to go where you go — a small friend, to be
shared with few or many just the two of you in sweet meditation."

Carl Sandburg (1878–1967)
  American poet, biographer, guitar balladeer.
  The Guitar dedicated to Andres Segovia

"He is made one with nature: there is heard
His voice in all her music, from the moan
of thunder to the song of night's sweet bird."

Percy Bysshe Shelley (1792–1822)
  Adonais (elegy to Keats) 1821
  Shelley, the English poet, died at age 30 by drowning
  during a storm in a collision between his
  small schooner and a *felucca* (fishing smack)
  in the Ligurian Sea while enroute to Leghorn
  (Livorno), Italy, to greet an old friend.

Pictured is a *zanza*: half a hollowed pump-
kin with wood sound board and small metal
tongues to be plucked by a player's fingers.
Made by the Ibos of Nigeria, who inhabit
the vast tropical rain forest of the Niger river
delta.

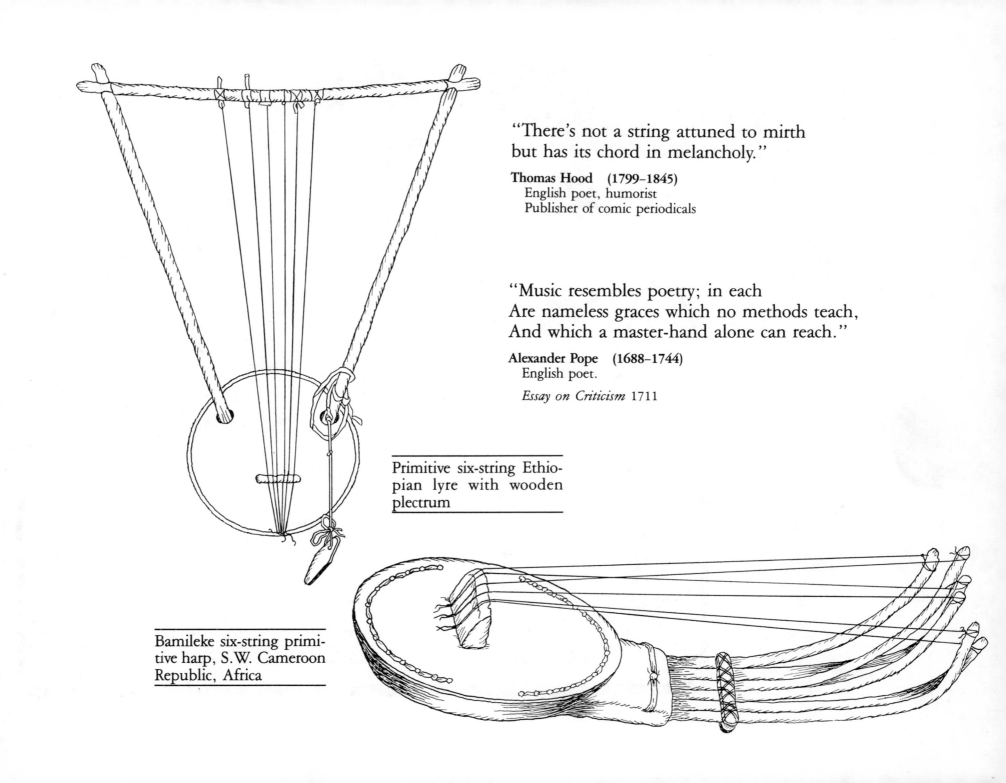

"There's not a string attuned to mirth
but has its chord in melancholy."

Thomas Hood   **(1799–1845)**
English poet, humorist
Publisher of comic periodicals

"Music resembles poetry; in each
Are nameless graces which no methods teach,
And which a master-hand alone can reach."

Alexander Pope   **(1688–1744)**
English poet.

Essay on Criticism 1711

Primitive six-string Ethio-
pian lyre with wooden
plectrum

Bamileke six-string primitive harp, S.W. Cameroon
Republic, Africa

"For Orpheus' lute was strung with poets' sinews, whose olden touch could soften steel and stones, make tigers tame and huge leviathans forsake unsounded depths to dance on sands."

William Shakespeare
The Two Gentlemen of Verona
First Folio 1623

Adapted from *The Concert*,
a painting by Lorenzo Costa,
Bologna, Italy: 1460–1535

Pocket fiddle called a Kit, 16 inches long, 18th C. to early 19th.

Kaspar Tieffenbrucker, The World's Greatest Lute Maker (1514–1571)

A noted Bavarian master lute maker in Nice,
France, where he was known as Gaspard
Duiffopruggar. He created the finest lutes the
world has ever seen. Their ribs were thinner
than 1/32", and so sensitive they trembled in
response to sounds as slight as the human voice.
Kaspar's instruments were as light as bird
wings. A choice piece of the luthier's art was his
viola da gamba crafted for France's young king,
François I. Its elaborate marquetry work features
a bird's-eye view of Paris made of varying inlaid
woods. Above it sits Saint Luke atop a billowing
cloud, in floral rococo splendor with a sacred
bull. — *B.B.*

"I was alive in the woods:
I was cut down by the cruel ax.
While I lived I was silent:
In death I sweetly sing."

*Inscription on the fingerboard
of a viola da gamba* made by
Kaspar Tieffenbrucker

From a lithograph
of the period

India's Mysterious Music
starring Ravi Shankar
and the SITAR

Most visitors to India are baffled by its music. It is as much a mystery as that nation's cuisine. Understanding of the music (*sangita*) is extremely difficult because it is so intimately linked to religion and philosophy, which dates back to 1500 B.C.

"Our music needs hearing in silence," Ravi Shankar told noisy audiences of young psychedelics hailing the *sitar* at concerts in the late 60s. He explained that he was improvising and if good vibrations occurred he could produce better music. "It is based on true spiritual feeling." Listeners didn't like the critique. Now, no more noisesome audiences for Ravi. He has returned to *raga sangreet*. A *raga* is a precise melodic form with 72 *melas* (parent scales), on which 16,000 *ragas* are based. Originally, *ragas* were chanted hymns. Shankar explains the spirit of *raga* as improvising on complex rhythmic cycles, a sort of intellectual jam session. ". . . at the same time we keep the emotional aspect. Each time we play a *raga* it cannot be 100 percent the same as a time before." Performance can be slow, medium, or fast tempo; serious devotional, erotic — depends on situation and time alloted: 15 minutes to several hours on the same piece. Of Indian classical music, Shankar says, "It is not like taking something from the outside. It is within the framework, based on a foundation of what the musicians have learned." When not playing strictly regulated *ragas*, he experiments with jazz on the sitar. "If I played Bach that would be disturbing, just a gimmick. I have never done that." He is too old now to start — 65 and still counting. *Vatya-shastra*, an ancient encyclopedia of music, dated within 200 BC and 400 AD, explains Indian rhythm and measure, and defines sound. It was considered then and still is considered either as *unstruck*, the vibration of ether, inaudible to man but delightful to gods, or as *struck*, man-made music that reflects universal laws, the result of mating physical breath with fires of intelligence, in connection to the god Brahma, who originated directly from the Supreme Being. Need I say more? — *B.B.*

"It is fascinating to watch an accomplished sitar (stringed instrument) player and drummer work together, for here the essence of all Indian music comes clear. The sitarist announces a simple little melody, the drummer a simple rhythm. Then they go to work on it, varying its rhythm, its structure in every imaginable way except harmonically, since Indian music works in unison or in simple following phrases but not through harmony. The complications increase, the artistry is exquisite, and those in the know smile and nod and snap their fingers in sheer joy."

Bradford Smith (1909–1964)
American journalist, biographer, professor: Columbia, Bennington: USA; St. Paul's, Imperial: Japan. World War II: chief, Central Pacific operations, USA Office of War Information. Co-director (with wife), Quaker International Center, New Delhi, India (3 years).

Portrait of India 1962

INDIA'S
MUSICAL
INSTRUMENTS

India's *strings: vina*, closest to our lute; *sitar*, seven strings plus 13 sympathetics; *tanpura*, accompanist of vocalists; *sarangi*, *andesraj* (akin to violin). *Winds*: conches, horns, flutes (straight, transverse). *Reeds*: *shanai*, *nagasvaram* (akin to oboe). *Percussion*: *tablā bāyan* (small kettledrums), *mridangam* (large, two-headed drum); cymbals, bells, and anklet bells for dancers. There are no keyboard instruments as Indian music has no exact tones.

Yehudi Menuhin
The Music of Man 1979
with Curtis W. Davis

"For the Indian, the individual note, with all its inflections and colors, equates the idea of personal salvation, of resignation, and acceptance."

"To me Indian music is like a river, ever-fluid and subtly changing, whereas European music is like a building, carefully structured upon constant principles."

"Their music does not favor sharp contrasts of mood as ours does; it can remain in one mode for an hour or more. It is meant to create a state of being, not put the listener through an emotional wringer."

This illustration is not, as one might at first think, a portrait of Gene Shalit on a bad morning on the *Today Show*, wearing a slew of Willard's hats. Hindus essentially are monotheists, but worship many of God's lieutenants. Foreigners visiting India soon become accustomed to garish representations of them — in plaster, carved wood, or stone. Kali usually is the best-equipped with extra appendages, and one favorite god, Ganesh, sports an elephant head, his own having been chopped off by his father Siva, the most feared of the emissary gods, who also is well hung with arms and legs, well entwined with serpents. "Never an easy one to get along with," states a tourist guide book. — *B.B.*

This temple carving of Hindu god, Siva, is at Madurai, in southern India, near the tip, 1400 miles south of Delhi, the capital. Siva is the patron god of Madurai and his Meenakshi Temple has a Hall of a Thousand Pillars, many of which play musical notes when struck.

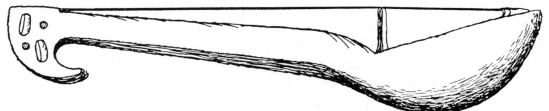

"My paramount object in this struggle is to save the Union, and is not either to save or destroy slavery. If I could save the Union without freeing any slave, I would do it; and if I could do it by freeing all the slaves, I would do it; and if I could save it by freeing some and leaving others alone, I would also do that."

Abraham Lincoln   (1809–1865)
  16th U.S. president, Republican.
  Letter to Horace Greeley, 22 August 1862

A famous composer for the banjo was Frederic Delius (1862–1934), friend of Gauguin, Ravel, Munch, and Strindberg. Banjo music is woven through Delius's opera *Koanga* (1895-7), about slaves on a Mississippi plantation.

George Gershwin used banjo music in his famous folk opera *Porgy and Bess*.

Primitive ancestor of the banjo, from Dahomey, a leading African shipping port of slaves to the Americas and the Carribean lands in the 1880s.

"I know only two tunes.
One of them is *Yankee Doodle*.
And the other isn't."

Ulysses Simpson Grant **(1822–1885)**
American Civil War Union general
and 18th president of the United States.

The banjo differs from all other fretted instruments. Its resonator is an open-back hoop of wood or metal over which is stretched either plastic or a fine-grain animal skin (calf, lamb, or kid).

Farland, a banjo virtuoso of the 1880s played banjo sonatas adapted from some composed by Bach for the unaccompanied violin.

Eddie Peabody was the master banjoist of modern times, in vaudeville and musical revues.

Adapted from a primitive painting by a slave of the period.

"Yankee Doodle,
keep it up,
Yankee Doodle Dandy;
Mind the music
and the step,
And with the girls
be handy."

popular song
by Edward Bangs
ca. 1775

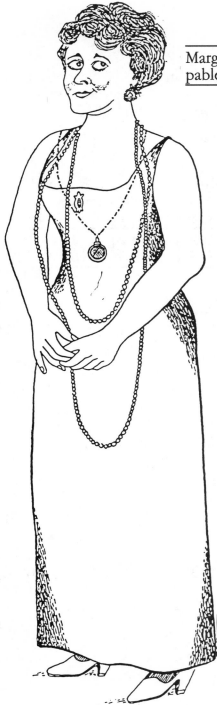

Margaret Dumont, the Marx Bros.' unflappable straight woman.

"Straight women always get it in the neck."

Roberta Louise Light (1922–   )
American poet, novelist, ex-showgirl: Billy Rose's Diamond Horseshoe and Ringling Bros. and Barnum & Bailey Circus; straight woman, famed vaudeville act, Herman Hyde & Co., musical parody. Mother of "five only children," and wife of an ex-circus clown, author-artist.

Julius (Groucho) Marx (1890–1977)
Comedian, stage, films, television.

"He was interested in playing the plucking harp which I hated. I don't know. I didn't like it. When we did the pictures later and I'd have to watch them, I'd leave the theater until the harp bit was over. I was glad he could play so well but the harp is not my instrument."

Richard Anobile (1947–   )
The Marx Brothers Scrap Book 1973

as Captain Jeffrey T. Spaulding, Paramount film *Animal Crackers* 1930

"Wherever it came from, the musical came with its hair mussed and with an innocent, indolent, irreverent look on its bright, bland face. It has an air about it of having strolled in from the street with a few tricks up its sleeve, and if everybody would relax, please, it would do its best to pass the time whimsically. Harpo Marx looks like a musical comedy."

Walter Kerr (1913–   )
    Theater critic, essayist
    Theatrical review, New York
    Herald-Tribune 1 Sept. 1963

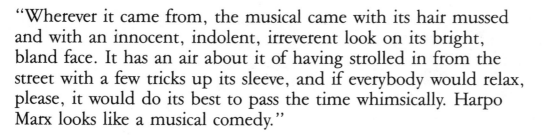

The Marx Bros.

| Chico (Leonard) 1887–1961 |
| Harpo (Arthur) 1888–1964 |
| Groucho (Julius) 1890–1977 |
| Gummo (Milton) 1892– |
| Zeppo (Herbert) 1901–1979 |

"Music is a science that would have us laugh, and sing, and dance."

Guillaume de Machaut (c. 1300–1377)
    French poet, musician, with 30 years service as secretary to the adventurous John of Luxembourg, king of Bohemia, accompanying him on 20 battles and 100 tourneys.

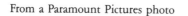

From a Paramount Pictures photo

Folk guitarist,
Bruskie Willits,
Bandana, Kentucky

"A guitar has moonlight in it."

James M. Cain   (1892–   )
American novelist.

Serenade 1937

Quitara, a Greek word, adopted by the Arabs in 1000 A.D. for their lute.

"My wife died in 1961. Ever since then my guitar has been my woman and my whiskey. Someday I'll die but you will remember me, my love. You will remember my song."

Don Eppemenio Valdex   (1890–   )
Retired *sovador* (chiropractor).

Interview at age 88, from the *Grass Roots People* by Nancy Wood, Harper & Row, NYC

The woods of a guitar: tiger maple, jacaranda, Peruvian mahogany, ebony, Sitka spruce, Brazilian or Indian rosewood.

Largest professional jazz guitar: 1951 Gibson Super 400. Grand-daddy of modern guitars: Washburn, arch-top and round-hole, 1887.

"Nuthin' much happened in Luckenbach this month,
'cept the potato chip man came by.
Then there was the moon.
We try to tell folks who come by here to look at our town
What a big mean moon we have
But nobody'd believe it.
And last night it showed off.
The greatest ever.
It just hung there, darin' you to look at it . . ."

Hondo Crouch
    Mayor, Luckenbach, Texas; gui-
    tarist, composer, balladeer.

    Luckenbach Moon 1976

Blue Grass guitars are called
Dreadnaughts.

"Bluegrass pickers have been havin' tailgate parties
since way back before there was tailgates."

Jake Vest
    American cartoonist
    That's Jake, a panel cartoon The
    Orlando (Fla.) *Sentinel*, Tribune
    Media Services, Inc.

Max Gordon, famed
Broadway producer,
couldn't understand how
Andrés Segovia could
earn a living just playing
guitar. "It is very
simple," he replied, "I
just sit down out on the
stage and play Bach and
Beethoven on my guitar,
and people pay to come
in and hear me play. I
keep busy: Carnegie
Hall, Paris Conservatory
of Music, Leipzig, Royal
Concert Hall, in
London." "My God!"
said Max. "It's just
one-night stands with a
banjo."

Charles Doss
American journalist, columnist
The Christian Science Monitor

". . . our enjoyment of music is not always wholly contingent upon its intrinsic beauty. As we grow older, we tend to idealize and romanticize a good bit . . . convinced that many good things happened to us in, say, 1954, while Bill Haley's Comets were making a lot of racket in the background, it's quite probable that we'll have a warm affection for 'Rock Around the Clock', . . . possibly the most atrocious song in the history of the earth.

In the fifties a song kicking around the juke boxes, 'Shh-boom,' featured lyrics somewhat less than sensational. The chorus went, "Shh-boom, shh-boom; Yah duh duh duh duh duh, duh, duh, duh, duh, duh, Shh-boom," which of curse is sheer idiocy.

Surely there can be nothing in all those 'duh duh duhs' that registers upon my heart as sweet music. It's just that I was *young* in 1955, and I was in love for the first and only time in my life. As this certain girl and I walked through the village of Lingayen, I happened by the merest chance to hear the strains of *Shh-boom* blaring from a kiosk. And at that instant it sprang to life in my smitten heart with all the power and beauty of a Tchaikovsky."

"You have to blame Thomas Alva Edison for today's rock'n'roll. He invented electricity."

Stan Getz (1927–   )
 Tenor saxaphone jazz musician.

"Electric guitars are an abomination.
Whoever heard of an electric violin?
An electric cello?
Or for that matter, an electric singer?"

Andrés Segovia (1893–   )
 Concert guitarist.

The Beatles, Words Without Music 1968

"Music now is so foolish that
I am amazed. Everything wrong
is permitted, and no attention
is paid to what the old generation
wrote as composition."

Samuel Scheidt (1587–1654)
 German organist, composer.

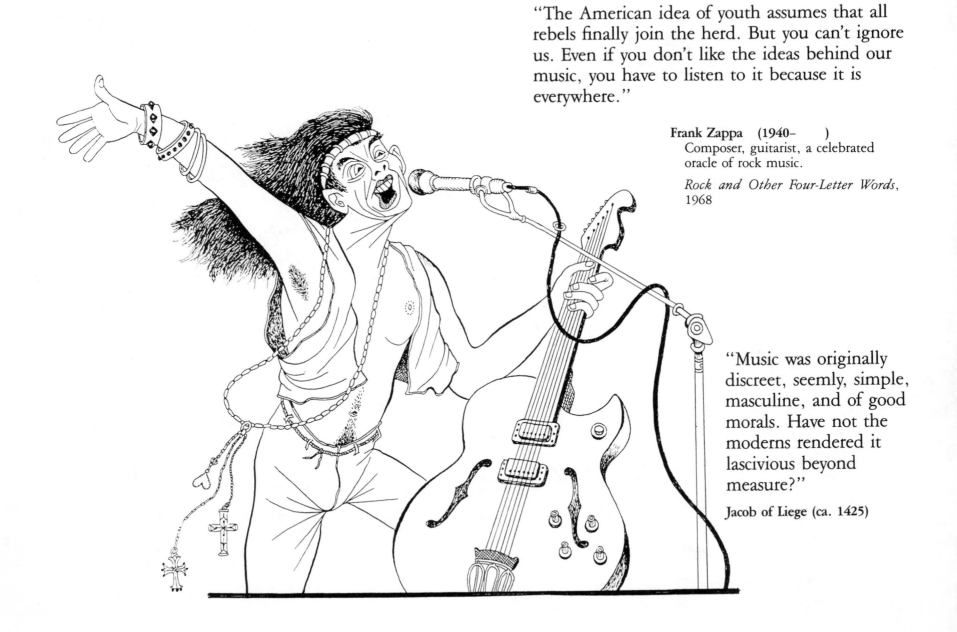

"The American idea of youth assumes that all rebels finally join the herd. But you can't ignore us. Even if you don't like the ideas behind our music, you have to listen to it because it is everywhere."

Frank Zappa (1940–   )
Composer, guitarist, a celebrated oracle of rock music.

Rock and Other Four-Letter Words, 1968

"Music was originally discreet, seemly, simple, masculine, and of good morals. Have not the moderns rendered it lascivious beyond measure?"

Jacob of Liege (ca. 1425)

"I love Beethoven,
especially the poems."

Richard Starkey, Jr. (1940–   )
aka: Ringo Starr, the Beatles' famous drummer.

"Stark contrast between a constant background noise and an irregular jumping movement always has an extraordinary effect on man. In the magical world of music it represents struggle of good and evil."

French author René Clemencic
Old Musical Instruments 1968

bowing 3

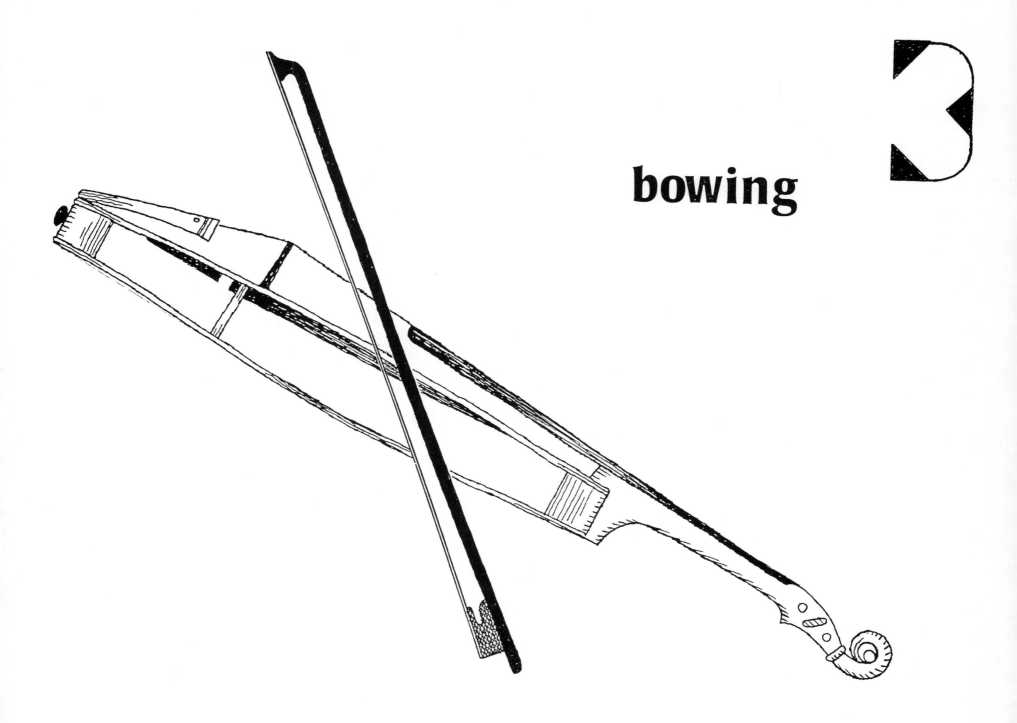

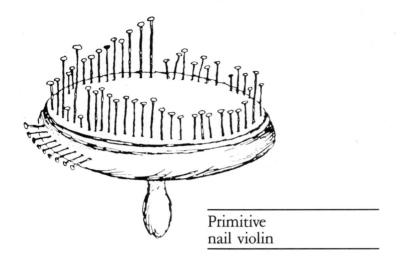

Primitive
nail violin

"O manes of my ancestors
O spirits of those watching over our people
Flow into me like water
Blow through me like a wind
And assist me to single out
The workers of evil spells in this village."

Song of an *Azande* witch-doctor,
Belgian Congo, central Africa.

John Latouche / André Cauvin *Congo* 1945

"It haunts me, the passage of time. I think time is a merciless thing.
I think life is a process of burning oneself out and time is the fire that
burns you. But I think the spirit of man is a good adversary."

Tennessee Williams   (1912–1983)
   American playwright

"Music is a beautiful opiate if you
don't take it too seriously."

Henry Miller   (1891–1980)
   American *avant garde* writer.

The Air-Conditioned Nightmare 1945

"His music used to be original.
Now it is aboriginal."

Sir Ernest Newman   (1868–1959)
   English music critic

Musical Times, London July 1921

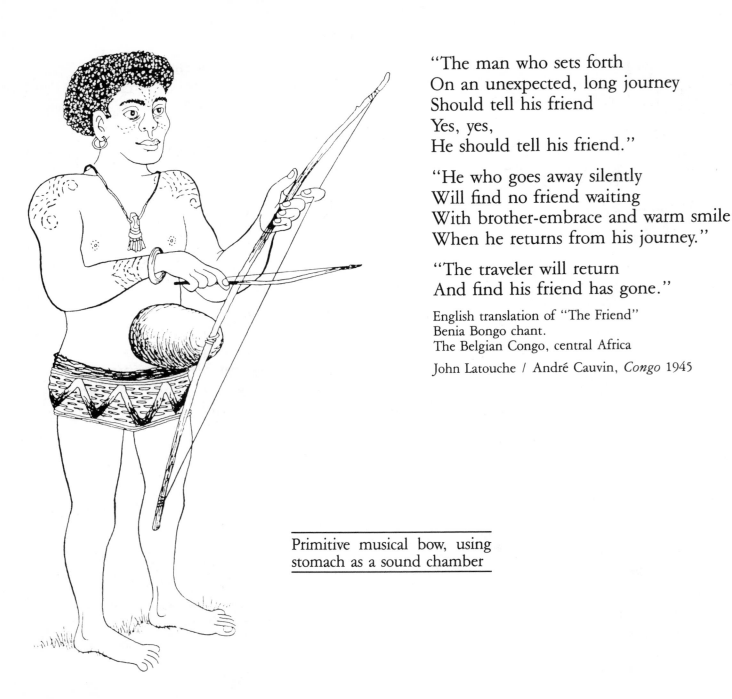

"The man who sets forth
On an unexpected, long journey
Should tell his friend
Yes, yes,
He should tell his friend."

"He who goes away silently
Will find no friend waiting
With brother-embrace and warm smile
When he returns from his journey."

"The traveler will return
And find his friend has gone."

English translation of "The Friend"
Benia Bongo chant.
The Belgian Congo, central Africa

John Latouche / André Cauvin, *Congo* 1945

Primitive musical bow, using
stomach as a sound chamber

"All knowledge is of itself of some value.
There is nothing so minute or inconsiderable
that I would not rather know it than not."

Samuel Johnson **(1709–1784)**
English writer, lexicographer.

James Boswell *The Life of Samuel Johnson* 1791

"Music was born free, and to win freedom is its destiny."

Ferruccio Busoni **(1866–1924)**
Italian composer, conductor, pianist.

"We have learnt that nothing is simple and rational except
what we ourselves have invented; that God thinks in terms
neither of Euclid nor of Riemann; that science has
'explained' nothing; that the more we know the more
fantastic the world becomes and the profounder the
surrounding darkness."

Aldous Leonard Huxley **(1894–1963)**
English author.

Views of Holland

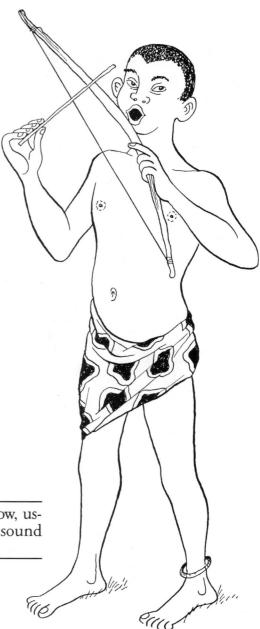

Primitive musical bow, using mouth as a sound
chamber

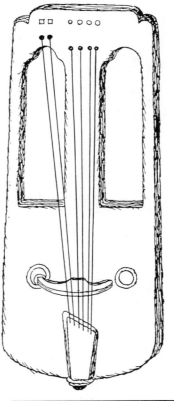

"In the Middle Ages alchemists dreamt of turning lead into gold. Musicians however longed to find an instrument that could sing like the human voice. The solution was the bowed string — to be stroked, not plucked."

Anonymous

". . . the argument that music vaguely of the period *must* express that period is unsound . . . because we are not listening with the ears of that period."

James Agate **(1877–1947)**
English writer.

The Later Ego (Published, 1951)

Welsh crwth:
Middle Ages lyre

9th century crwth

Viola da braccio

"How shall we sing the Lord's song in a strange land?"

The Holy Bible: Psalms 137:4

"Ever since de apple in de Garden of Eve,
Man always foolin' wid things
    that cause him to grieve . . .
But not since de doomsday in old Babylon
Did he fool wid anything so diabolical
    as de cyclotron.
So, if you wish to avoid
    de most uncomfortable trip to Paradise,
You will be scientific and take my advice —
Leave de atom alone.
Leave de atom alone.
Don't get smart alecksy
Wid de galaxy.
"Leave atom alone . . ."

Edgar Yipsel Harburg   (1898–1981)
  Famed writer of Broadway musicals,
  composer.
Self-styled "minstrel and lyrical historian."

The musical *Jamaica*.

Minnesingers were Germanic troubadours,
singers of love songs, in the 12th and 13th
centuries. They were merchants and trades-
men, mostly of aristocratic origin. Wagners
opera *Tannhauser* features them.

Minnesinger fiddle

After an engraving by Hans Memling

Viol da Gamba
of 15th Century
Spain

"Come sing me a bawdy song; make me merry."

Shakespeare
Henry IV. III.iii.

"People who lead a lonely existence always have something on their minds that they are eager to talk about."

Anton Pavlovich Chekhov   (1860–1904)
Russian dramatist, story writer.

"I was lonesomer than Crusoe's goat."

O. Henry (William S. Porter)   (1862–1910)
American short story writer.

"An artist is always alone — if he *is* an artist . . . the artist needs loneliness."

Henry Miller   (1891–1980)
American novelist, social activist.

Tropic of Cancer 1934

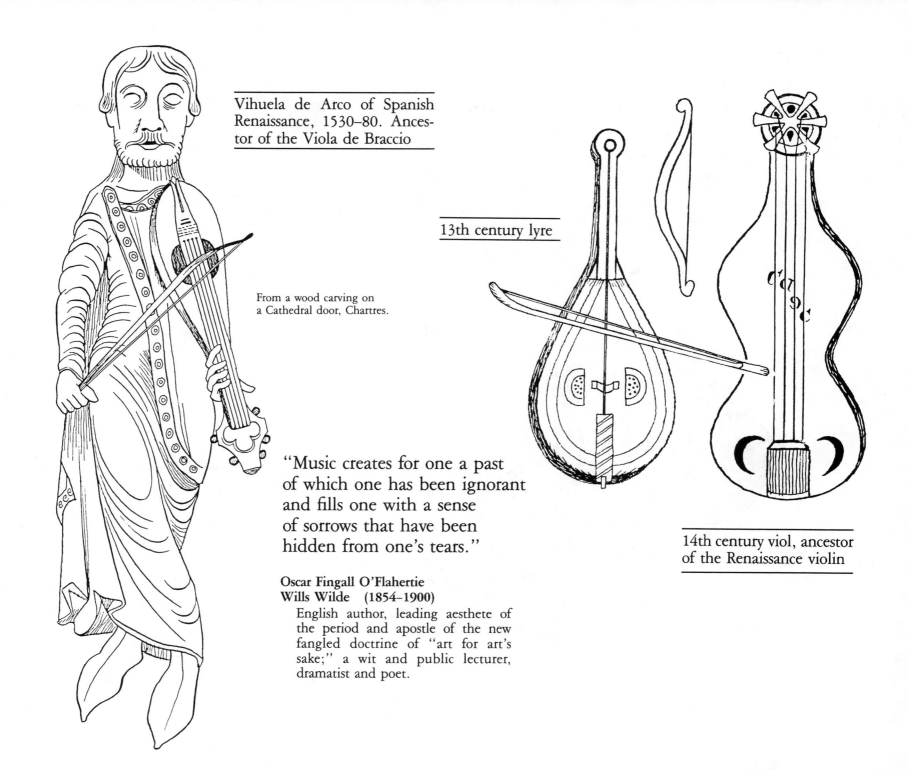

Vihuela de Arco of Spanish Renaissance, 1530–80. Ancestor of the Viola de Braccio

From a wood carving on a Cathedral door, Chartres.

13th century lyre

"Music creates for one a past of which one has been ignorant and fills one with a sense of sorrows that have been hidden from one's tears."

Oscar Fingall O'Flahertie Wills Wilde (1854–1900)
English author, leading aesthete of the period and apostle of the new fangled doctrine of "art for art's sake;" a wit and public lecturer, dramatist and poet.

14th century viol, ancestor of the Renaissance violin

After a period engraving

Giovanni Battista VIOTTI
(1755–1824)

"Everything he touches turns to music."

Robert Alexander Schumann **(1810–1856)**
   German romantic composer, pianist.

"To teach is to learn."

   Ancient Japanese proverb.

"The art of teaching is the art of assisting discovery."

Mark Van Doren **(1894–1972)**
   American poet, critic, English professor.

Musical ancestor of many 20th century violinists. Taught Jacques Pierre Joseph Rode (Napoleon's violinist), who in turn taught Joseph Bohm. A pupil of his, Jakob Dont, was violin master of Leopold Auer, whose pupils included some of the brightest violinist stars of our time: Mischa Elman, Jascha Heifetz, Nathan Millstein, Mishel Piastro, and Efrem Zimbalist. Viotti himself was taught by his father, a blacksmith.

"If I had a child who wanted to be a teacher,
I would bid him Godspeed as if he were going to a war.
For indeed the war against prejudice, greed, and ignorance
is eternal, and those who dedicate themselves to it
give their lives no less because they may live to see
some fraction of the battle won."

James Hilton   (1900–1954)
  British author, best-known
  for *Lost Horizon*

". . . some person — a teacher — he could tell me:
'Look at the music.' He'd want me to read one note,
and I'd see the whole page . . . ain't never learned
to read one note after the other . . . I'd see the whole
thing . . . and from there on I'd be on my own . . .
And that's the way it has to be . . . Ain't no one can
write down the feeling you have to have."

Sidney Bechet   (1897–1950)
  Jazz musician, early innovator:
  soprano saxophone, master of blues and ragtime.

  Growing Up, an autobiography 1960

"They dined on mince, with slices of quince,
Which they ate with a runcible spoon,
And hand in hand, on the edge of the sand,
They danced by the light of the moon."

Edward Lear (1812–1888)
English artist, humorist,
maker of foolish limericks.

The Owl and the Pussy Cat

"Hey diddle, diddle,
The cat and the fiddle,
The cow jumped over the moon;
The little dog laughed
To see such sport,
And the dish ran away with the spoon."

Familiar old nursery rhyme. Earliest
printed form: ca 1765.

AFTER
Randolph Caldecott

"Ye harpe on the stryng that geuth no melody."

John Heywood **(1497–1580)**
English dramatist.

Proverbs 1546

"Harp not on that string."

William Shakespeare
Richard III, IV.iv.

"And sure the Eternal Master found
The single talent well employed."

Samuel Johnson **(1709–1784)**
English writer, lexicographer.

On the Death of Mr. Levett

"The man that has no music in himself.
Nor is not moved with concord of sweet sounds.
Is fit for treasons, stratagems, and spoils."

William Shakespeare
The Merchant of Venice, V.i.

Tromba Marina is not a trumpet, but a monochord of one long gut string, and a forefather of the cello. Before the 16th century it was called *Deum log* or *trumscheit* because of its peculiar vibrating bridge, which also gave a brassy timbre. Nuns in convents substituted the *tramscheit* for the trumpet's forbidden masculinity, so then it was called the nun's fiddle, or *Nonnengeige*.

Some musical scholars consider the hurdy-gurdy to be a mechanical fiddle because its melody strings are rubbed — not by a bow, but by a resined wooden wheel revolving inside the instrument's case, being turned by a crank. Stopping rods, keys, and tangents substitute for a player's fingers. This odd music maker was known as early as the 10th century. The first picture of it appeared in the 12th. Six-feet long then, and played by two men: one, the cranker, the other working the rods. During the following century the hurdy-gurdy became portable.

Adapted from a 16th century
etching by Jacques Bellange

"Let a short Act of Parliament be passed, placing all street musicians outside the protection of the law, so that any citizen may assail them with stones, sticks, knives, pistols, or bombs, without incurring any penalties — except, of course, in the case of the instrument itself being injured. For Heaven forbid that I should advocate any disregard of the sacredness of property . . ."

George Bernard Shaw (1856–1950)
London Morning Leader,
27 November 1893

"These three take crooked ways:
carts, boats, and musicians."

Ancient Hindu saying

"If any person or persons . . . commonly
called Fidlers or Minstrels shall be
taken playing, fidling, or making music,
in any Inn, Alehouse, or Tavern . . .
every such person shall be adjudged
Rogues, vagabonds, and sturdy beggars
. . . and be punished as such."

Act of Parliament, England, 1642

"The loveliest tune imaginable becomes vulgar
and insupportable as soon as the public begins
to hum it and the hurdy-gurdies make it their own."

Joris Karl Huysmans   (1848–1907)
French novelist, disciple of Emile Zola.

Against the Grain 1884

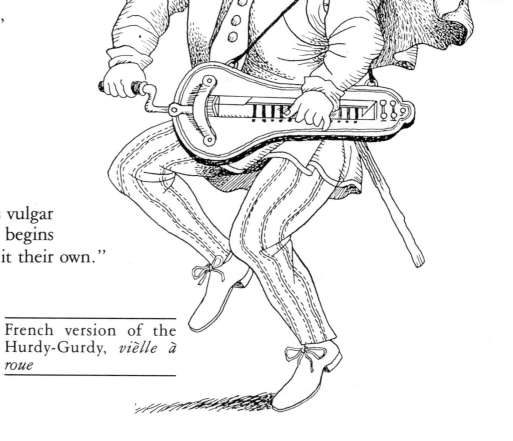

French version of the
Hurdy-Gurdy, *vièlle à
roue*

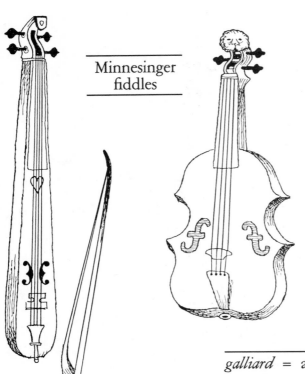

Minnesinger
fiddles

"For the good are always the merry,
Save by an evil chance,
And the merry love the fiddle,
And the merry love to dance."

William Butler Yeats
  Irish poet, playwright.

  "The Fiddler of Dooney" 1899

galliard = a lively triple-time dance
coranto = a running, gliding dance
sink-a-pace = cinque-pace, a five-paces
figure
make water = take a leak, pee

"Why dost thou not go to church
in a galliard and come home in
a coranto? My very walk should
be a jig. I would not so much
as make water but in a sink-a-pace."

William Shakespeare

Twelfth Night 1601

"Always those that dance must pay the music."

John Taylor **(1580–1653)**
English pamphleteer,
commonly called
"The Water Poet"

Taylor's Feast 1638

"Fiddle, n. An instrument
to tickle human ears
by friction of a horse's tail
on the entrails of a cat."

Ambrose Gwinett Bierce **(1842–1914)**
American journalist, author.

The Devil's Dictionary 1911

"Fate's a fiddler, Life's a dance."

William Ernest Henley **(1849–1903)**
English poet, critic, editor.

Double Ballade of Life and Fate

After Thomas Rowlandson

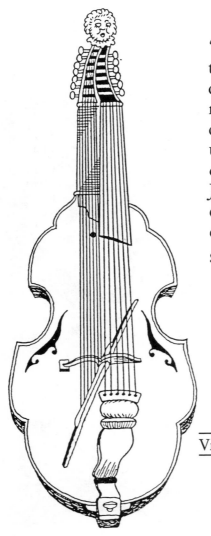

"The wonderful thing about playing chamber music is that we're not constantly playing the same ten concertos. We have this great, limitless literature to nourish us. Most of the great composers loved writing chamber music more than symphonic music. They were usually writing for each other — as Mozart and Haydn did with each other and Brahms did with Joseph Joachim and Clara Schumann. With almost every great composer, one finds that their very best work is their chamber music."

Sharon Robinson (1949–   )
American cellist, Kalichstein-Laredo-Robinson Trio
The Orlando (Fla.) *Sentinel*, interview Stephen Wigler.

Viola d'amore

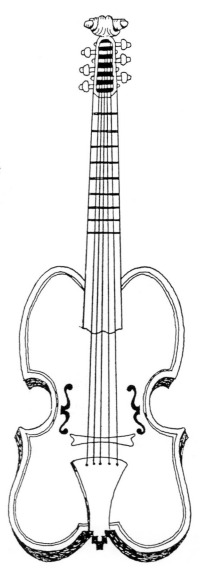

Double bass
Viol, Violone

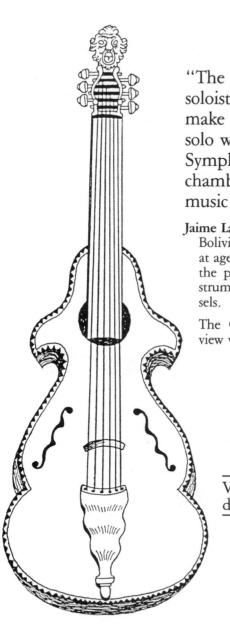

"The common wisdom was that if you couldn't make it as a soloist, you became a chamber-music player. And if you couldn't make it as chamber player, you went into an orchestra. Playing a solo with an orchestra — even one as great as the London Symphony — just isn't as satisfying for a musician as playing chamber music. You have more control over things. Chamber music is real soul food. The other stuff is often just for show."

Jaime Laredo (1941–   )
Bolivian violinist, adopted American at age seven. First place, at age 17, in the prestigious Queen Elizabeth Instrumentalists Competition, in Brussels.

The Orlando (Fla.) *Sentinel*, interview with Stephen Wigler

Viola
da gamba

Viola
da bracello

"Music is like the ocean. The instrument
is an island — small or big."

Andrés Segovia (1893–   )
  Spanish guitar virtuoso.

There are no traces of musical bowing before the
8th century. By the 10th century bowing was
practiced from the Atlantic to the Pacific.

Chamorro boy on the island of Guam, playing the
one-string Belimbau-Tuyan, using as a sound chamber his stomach. His head rests on a wooden coconut
grater.

Primitive
string bows

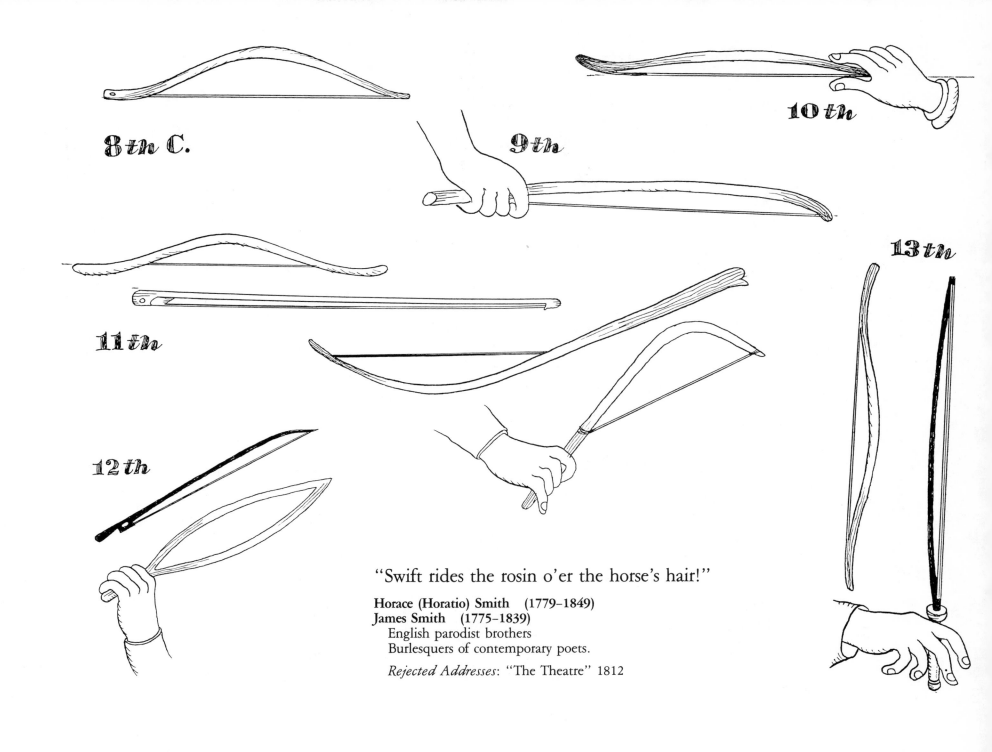

8th C.

9th

10th

11th

12th

13th

"Swift rides the rosin o'er the horse's hair!"

Horace (Horatio) Smith   (1779–1849)
James Smith   (1775–1839)
  English parodist brothers
  Burlesquers of contemporary poets.

Rejected Addresses: "The Theatre" 1812

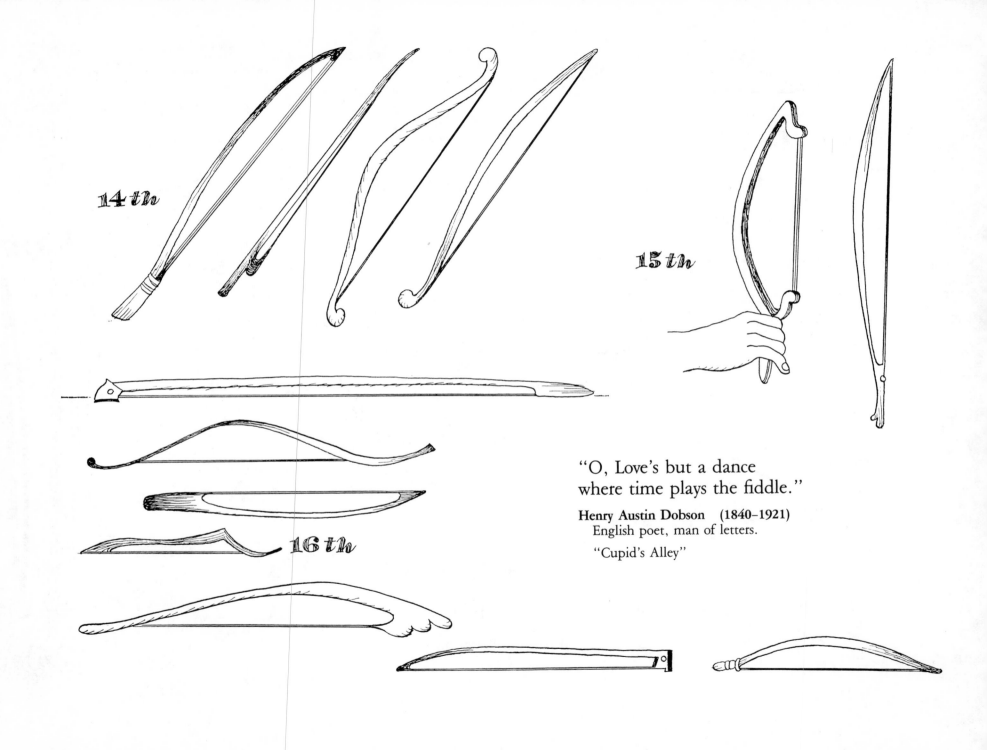

14th

15th

16th

"O, Love's but a dance
where time plays the fiddle."

Henry Austin Dobson   **(1840–1921)**
English poet, man of letters.

"Cupid's Alley"

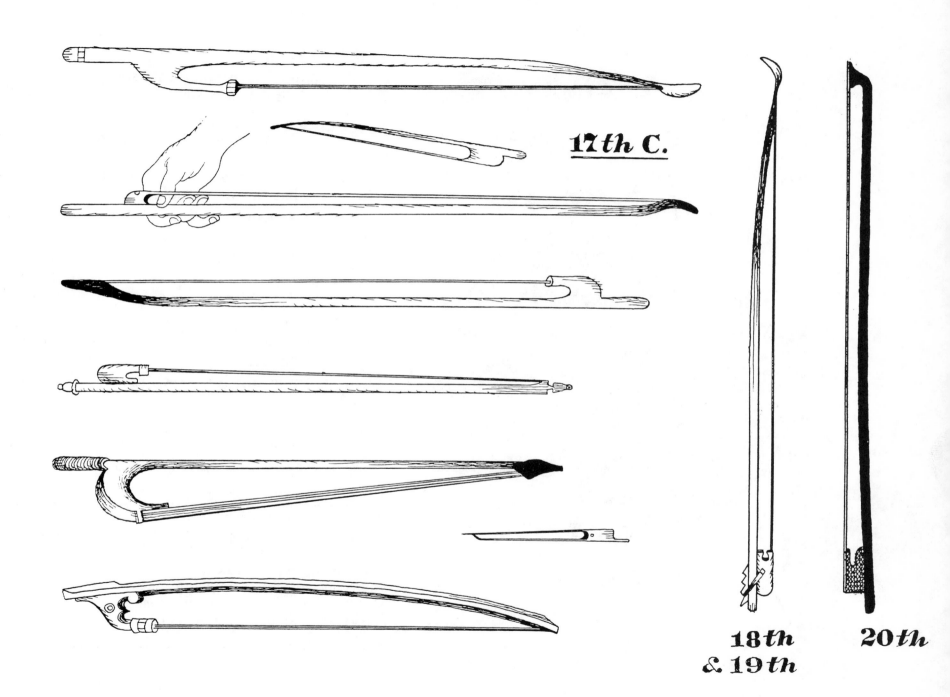

17th C.

18th
& 19th

20th

François TOURTE
(1747–1835)

"Is it not strange that sheep's guts should hale souls out of men's bodies?"

William Shakespeare
Much Ado About Nothing: quarto 1600

"The lesson of life is to believe what the years and centuries say against the hours."

James Reston   (1909–   )
   Scottish-born journalist,
   Political commentator
   The New York Times.

"The bitter and the sweet come from the outside, the hard from within, from one's own efforts. For the most part, I do the thing which my own nature drives me to do."

Albert Einstein   (1879–1955)
   German-Swiss theoretical physicist.

News Summary, 19 April 1955

This sorrowful Frenchman was the greatest bow maker of all time — responsible for its present length (29½"), elegant *cambé*, strength, and flexibility. He gave the bow a higher, heavier head to keep its hairs from touching the stick. Tourte's new bow allowed speedier, bouncing strokes, smoother legato, longer ccrescendos, stronger accents, super *sforzando* (forcing) of a note or chord.

"From this did Paganini comb the fierce Electric sparks, or to tenuity pull forth the inmost wailings of the wire — No catgut could swoon out so much soul."

Robert Browing **(1812–1889)**
English poet.

Red Cotton, Night-cap Country 1873

"He who plays the piano keeps sane."

Italian folk saying

"Audiences exist to be impressed, affected, startled, stunned, awed, delighted, to be confronted, confounded, and if necessary wrestled to the floor."

Charles Champlin **(1926–   )**
Film critic, *Los Angeles Times.*

Review: Robert Altman's
McCabe and Mrs. Miller

Niccolò **PAGANINI**
(1782–1840)

PAGANINI

A Super-skilled,
devilishly dynamic,
musical showman.

Niccolò Paganini, greatest violin virtuoso on earth. Did more to advance violin technique than anyone before him. Played mandolin at five, violin at seven, toured at thirteen. Extra sharp hearing, felt physical pain at loud speaking near him. Heard faint whispers at great distances. Ear for music so sensitive he could play completely in tune a violin completely out of tune. From age 14 to 17, practiced ten hours daily with only a pet spider for company. His concerts were musical fireworks displays. Fantastic runs, melodies played on one string accompanied by little-finger pluckings. Bounced his bow in lightning-swift alternation with left-hand pizzicatos. Played entire melodies on two different strings at once. Composed many pieces for G-string alone. Pioneered use of harmonics, tuned for special effects, exploited stacatto and pizzicato as never before. A true musical marvel!

London adored Paganini. Paris worshipped him. Vienna considered him a public idol, greater even than the giraffe presented to the court by the Pasha of Egypt.

Failure of his Paris gambling casino in 1836 hastened his death in 1840 from cancer of the larynx. A son, Achillino, inherited 80,000 lire.

"He that has a great Nose
thinks everybody is speaking of it."

Thomas Fuller   (1608–1661)
English clergyman, writer, wit.

Gnomologia

". . . a schnozzola, a nose with musical
and snoring attachments."

Jimmy Durante   (1893–1980)
American musical comedian:
nightclub, stage, tv, movies. His
trademark and nickname for an
oversize nose.

"If the nose of Cleopatra
had been a little shorter
the whole face of the world
would have been changed."

Blaise Pascal   (1623–1662)
French religious philosopher.

Pensées VI

(1731–1798)

From an 18th Century engraving

Short, misshapen and with a jib-topsail for a nose, Gaetano
Pugnani's entry on concert stages always set off a wave of merri-
ment. But his violin virtuosity — brilliant runs, double-triple
stops — left audiences breathless and very respectful. His skill as a
teacher was equally great. His star pupil was the great violinist
Giovanni Battista Viotti. — *B.B.*

"Ballonius speaks of a nose six times larger
than ordinary. Viewing the Roman celebrities,
we find that Numa, to whom was given the surname,
Pompilius, had a nose which measured six inches.
Plutarch, Lycurgus, and Solon had a similar
enlargement, as had all the kings of Italy
except Tarquin the Superb."

Dik Browne   (1916–   )
American comic-strip cartoonist.

Hagar the Horrible
©King Features Syndicate, Inc. NY/NY
The Orlando (Fla.) *Sentinel*
27 May 1985

George M. Gould, M.D., Walter L. Pyle, M.D.
American researchers of medical literature
Anomalies and Curiosities of Medicine 1896
Guiliemus Ballonius: *Opera Medica Omnia* 1762

The spike fiddle is found all over the Islamic world.

"Moorish music rang forth not only in the blossoming gardens watered by sibilant fountains, but indoors in the harem, and especially in the baths. Here musicians performed from the upper gallery for the delight of those dallying below. As the baths were one of the most popular places of assignation these unfortunate players were first blinded and then emasculated to remove them from temptation."

Yehudi Menuhin (1916–   )
Concert violinist, child prodigy.

The Music of Man 1979
with Curtis W. Davis

Mentioned as early as the 10th century, North Iranian district of Kurdistan.

"And the night shall be filled with music
And the cares that infest the day,
Shall fold their tents, like the Arabs,
And as silently steal away."

Henry Wadsworth Longfellow (1807–1882)
  American poet, professor modern
  languages: Harvard University.

  "The Day Is Done"
  from *Tales of a Wayside Inn* 1863

"No nightingale did ever chant
More welcome notes to weary bands
Of travelers in some shady haunt,
Among Arabian sands."

William Wordsworth (1770–1850)
  English poet.

  "The Solitary Reaper"

The rabab: most popular
spike fiddle of the Arabs

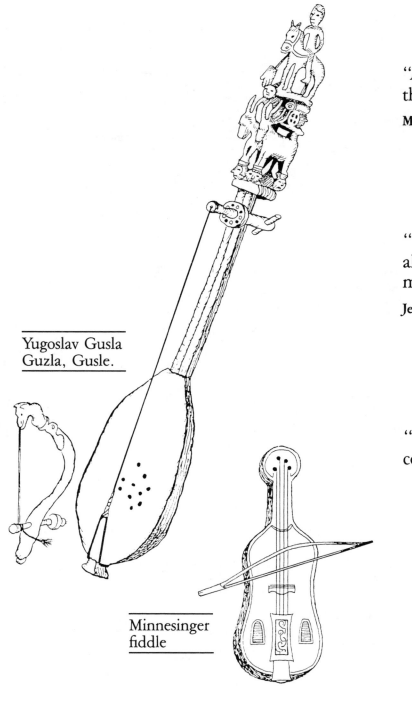

Yugoslav Gusla
Guzla, Gusle.

Minnesinger
fiddle

"A nation creates music —
the composer only arranges it."

Mikhail Ivanovich Glinka   (1803–1857)
Soviet composer.

Theatre Arts magazine June 1958

"Be on your guard because
alone of all the arts,
music moves all around you."

Jean Cocteau
French writer, visual artist.

Cock and Harlequin 1918

"Fiddlers, dogs, and flies
come to feasts uncalled."

Scottish proverb, ca. 1649

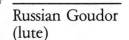

Russian Goudor
(lute)

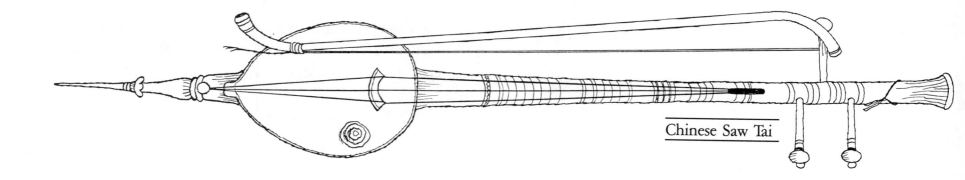

Chinese Saw Tai

The author's name
in Chinese characters
by Teddy T. K. Lee
Kong Kong

"For the Chinese, music was a tool to govern
the hearts of the people. It is said in China that
when there is music in the home, there is
affection between father and son, and when
music is played in public there is harmony
among the people."

Yehudi Menuhin (1916–   )
   American violinist, symphonic
   conductor, author.

The Music of Man 1979
with Curtis W. Davis

"Virtue is our favorite flower.
Music is the perfume of that flower."

Le Ly Kim (7th century B.C.)
   Chinese poet
   Ancient Chinese saying

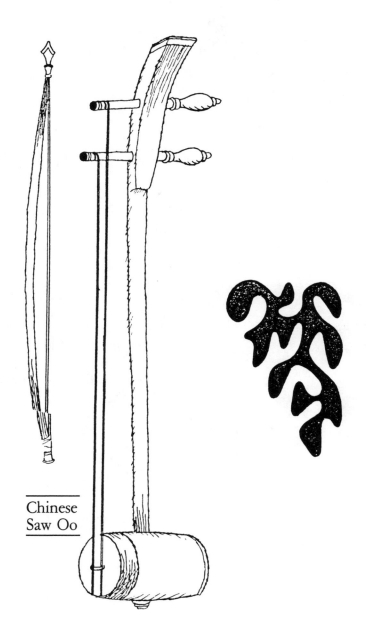

Chinese
Saw Oo

"I have a hankering to go back to the Orient and discard my necktie. Neckties strangle clear thinking."

Lin Yutang (1895–1976)
Chinese-American writer, philosopher.

News Summaries, 22 February 1954

"On the road to Mandalay,
Where the flyin' fishes play,
An' the dawn comes up like thunder
Outer China 'crost the Bay!"

Rudyard Kipling (1865–1936)
British author, born in Bombay.
Chronicler of adventures in India.

"Birds in their little nests agree
With Chinamen, but not with me."

Hilaire Belloc (1870–1953)
Joseph Hilaire Pierre Belloc
British author, born in France.
New Cautionary Tales on Food

Sarinda:
horsehair
or gut strings
favored by
leading commercial
caste, Khatri,
of North India.

Three main
groups: Bari, Bunjahis
and Sarin.

"Nothing great was ever achieved without enthusiasm."

Ralph Waldo Emerson **(1803–1883)**
American poet and essayist.

"And one is touched by something like reverence when one finds . . . a man who really knows on what stage he is playing, for what drama he has been cast."

Edmund Wilson **(1895–1972)**
American author; literary, social critic.

Night Thoughts in Paris 1922

The Sarangi is an instrument of North India. It comes from horse-breeding country in Central Asia.

There are four gut strings to be bowed and fifteen sympathetic strings.

It is hollowed from one block of wood. Waisted front is entirely covered with animal skin. Primitive forms still in use in Turkestan among Tatars and Kirghizes.

"I would sell my bread for marmalade."

Theophile Gautier **(1811–1872)**
French poet and miscellaneous writer

Caprices et zig-zags

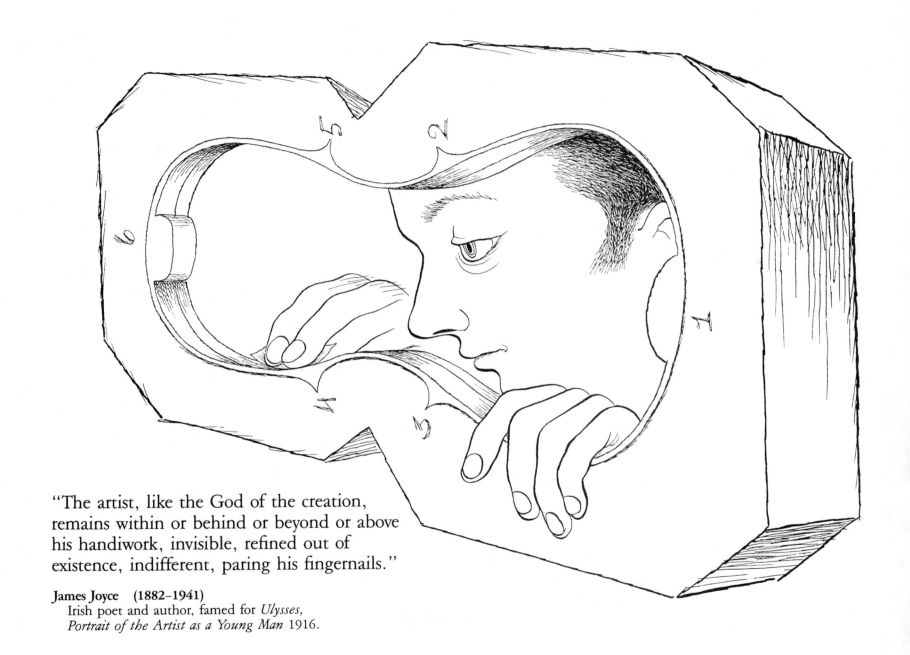

"The artist, like the God of the creation, remains within or behind or beyond or above his handiwork, invisible, refined out of existence, indifferent, paring his fingernails."

James Joyce **(1882–1941)**
  Irish poet and author, famed for *Ulysses,*
  Portrait of the Artist as a Young Man 1916.

"Many things difficult to design prove easy to performance."

Samuel Johnson **(1709–1784)**
English writer, lexicographer: *Rasselas XIII.*

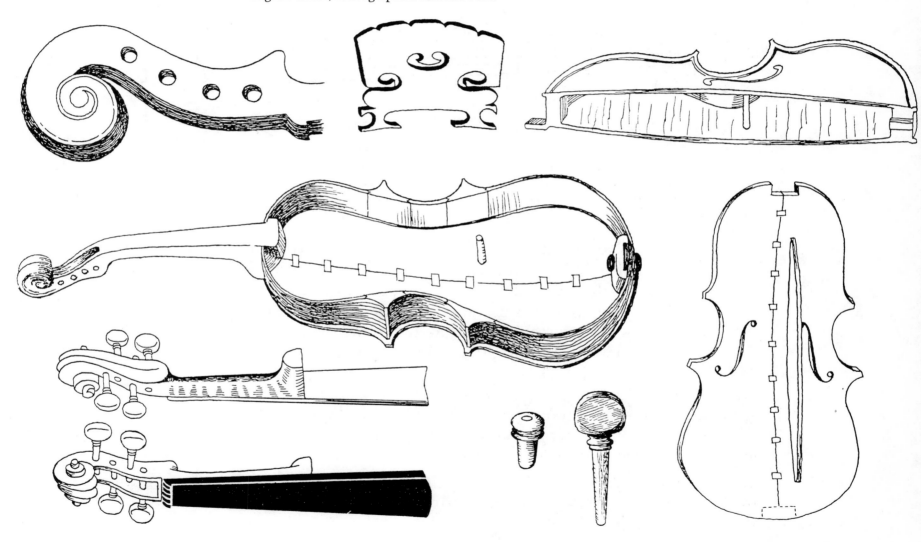

"No man is an Iland, intire of it selfe; every man is a peece
of the Continent, a part of the maine; if a Clod bee washed away
by the Sea, Europe is the lesse, as well as if a Promontorie
were, as well as if a Mannor of thy friends or of thine owne
were; any man's death diminishes me, because I am involved
in Mankinde; And therefore never send to know for whom the bell
tolls; It tolls for thee."

John Donne   **(1573–1631)**
  English poet and divine of the reigns of James I and Charles I

  Devotions Upon Emergent Occasions XVII. 1624.

"I can play the lute, violin, bagpipe, syrinx, harp, gigue, gittern, symphony, psaltery, organistrum, regals, tabor, and the rote. I can sing a song well and make tales and fables against any man. Then I can throw knives into the air, and catch them without cutting my fingers. I can do dodges with string, balance chairs, and make tables dance. I can throw a somersault and walk on my head."

Proud boast of a popular battlefield *jongleur*
known as the "Cleaver of Iron," during the
conquest of the Normans over the Saxons, 1066 AD.

"It is the fools and the knaves that make
the wheels of the world turn. They are the
world; those few who have sense or honesty
sneak up and down single, but never go in herds."

Sir George Savile **(1726–1784)**
English politician, Marquis of Halifax.

Political, Moral, and Miscellaneous Reflections 1750

Adrien Wettach aka GROCK, the Clown

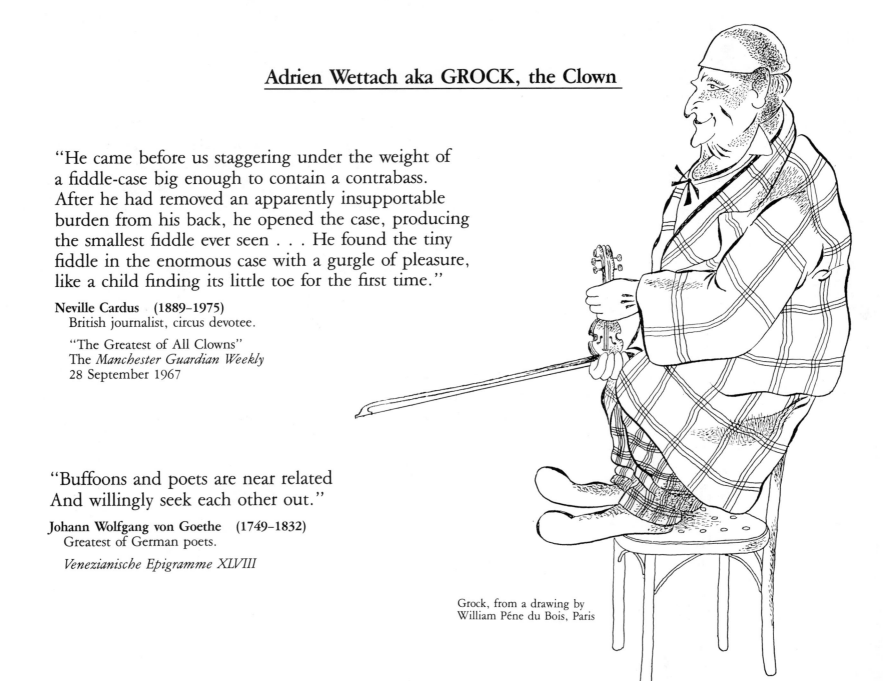

"He came before us staggering under the weight of
a fiddle-case big enough to contain a contrabass.
After he had removed an apparently insupportable
burden from his back, he opened the case, producing
the smallest fiddle ever seen . . . He found the tiny
fiddle in the enormous case with a gurgle of pleasure,
like a child finding its little toe for the first time."

Neville Cardus (1889–1975)
  British journalist, circus devotee.

  "The Greatest of All Clowns"
  The *Manchester Guardian Weekly*
  28 September 1967

"Buffoons and poets are near related
And willingly seek each other out."

Johann Wolfgang von Goethe (1749–1832)
  Greatest of German poets.

  Venezianische Epigramme XLVIII

Grock, from a drawing by
William Péne du Bois, Paris

"For God's sake give me the young man who has brains enough to make a fool of himself."

Robert Louis Balflour
Stevenson (1850–1894)
  British essayist, poet, and novelist, best-known for his novel *The Sea Cook*, finally titled *Treasure Island* 1881.

  Crabbed Age and Youth

"It's a good thing
to be foolishly gay
once in a while."

Horace (65–08 B.C.)
aka **Quintus Horatius Flaccus**
  Roman poet, second only to Virgil
  Carmina IV.xii.

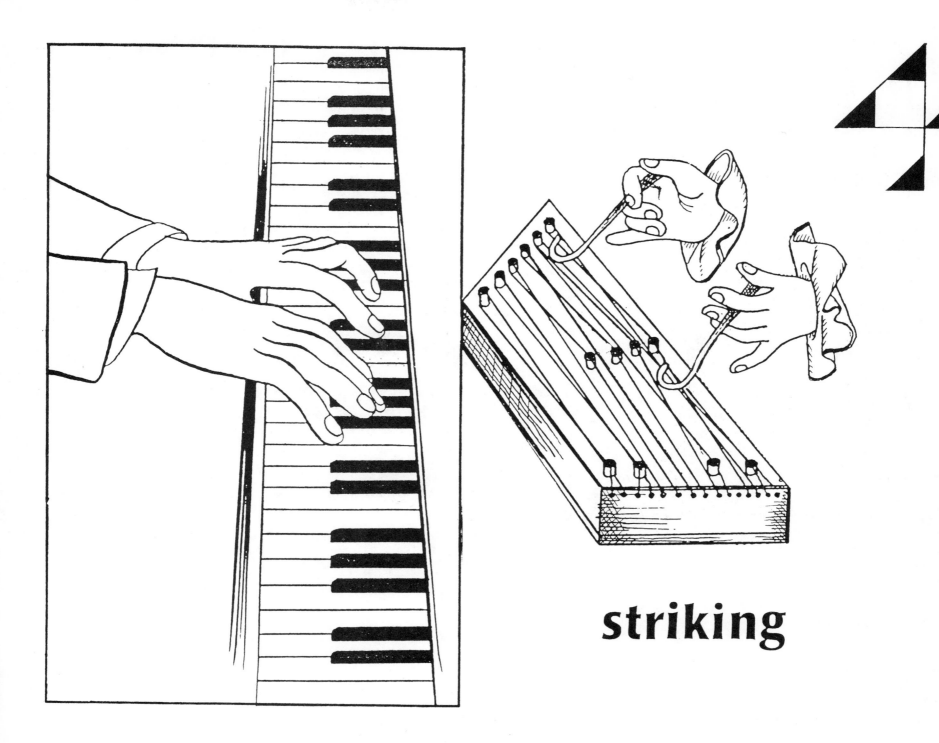

striking

"Most people wouldn't know music
if it came up and bit them on the ass."

Frank Zappa (1940–   )
American rock musician and composer.
Rolling Stone 1972

The dulcimer is ancient. Its
first record is a carved-stone
picture made in 667 B.C.,
found at the site of Nineveh, a
city of historic Assyria. It shows
king viewing a parade in
which a man with a stick
strikes the strings of an instrument hung from his neck. His
free hand's palm checks the
tone of the strings.

"With the greatest talent,
if you don't have discipline,
forget it; one day you will
fall apart."

Alexander Schneider (1908–   )
American violinist, conductor.

From a period engraving

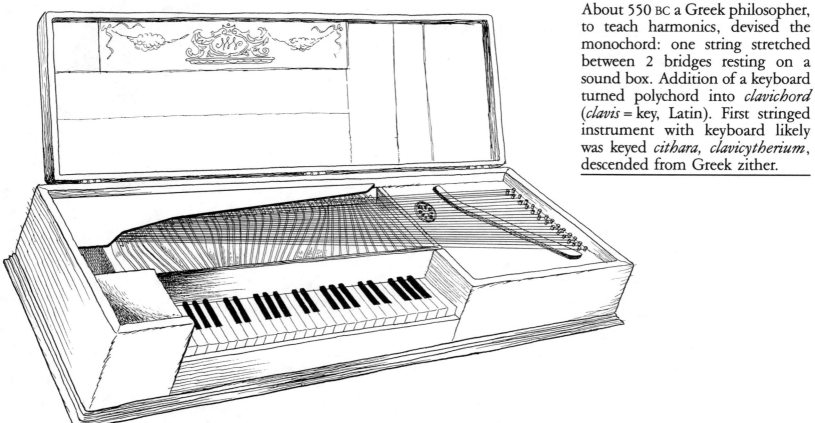

About 550 BC a Greek philosopher, to teach harmonics, devised the monochord: one string stretched between 2 bridges resting on a sound box. Addition of a keyboard turned polychord into *clavichord* (*clavis* = key, Latin). First stringed instrument with keyboard likely was keyed *cithara*, *clavicytherium*, descended from Greek zither.

"The isle is full of noises,
Sounds and sweet airs, that give delight and hurt not.
Sometimes a thousand twangling instruments
Will hum about mine ears; and sometimes voices,
That, if I then had wak'd after long sleep,
Will make me sleep again."

William Shakespeare
The Tempest III. ii. folio 1623

"You are beautiful and faded,
Like an opera tune
Played upon a harpsichord."

Amy Lowell (1874–1925)
  American poet, critic, lecturer.
  A Lady

"The sound of a harpsichord:
Two skeletons copulating
on a galvanised-tin roof."

Sir Thomas Beecham (1879–1961)
  English orchestra conductor.

"If music be the food of love, play on,
Give me excess of it; that surfeiting,
The appetite may sicken, and so die."

William Shakespeare
  English poet, player, playwright
  Twelfth Night I.i. 1601.

Harpsichord maker Bartolomeo Cristofori presents the world's first piano to his patron, Ferdinando del Medici, 1698, Florence.

"The pianoforte is the most important of all musical instruments: its invention was to music what the invention of printing was to poetry."

George Bernard Shaw
  "The Religion of the Pianoforte"
  The Fortnightly Review, London, Feb. 1894.

Henry Engelhardt Steinweg
(1797–1874)

"Respect the pianoforte! It gives a single man command over something complete in its ability to go from very soft to very loud in one and the same register it excels all other instruments. The trumpet can blare, but not sigh; the flute is contrary; the pianoforte can do both."

Ferruccio Benvenuto Busoni (1866–1924)
  Italian composer, pianist, orchestra conductor.

From a photograph mid-19th century

Heinrich Engelhardt Steinweg with his first piano, a small grand, built in the family kitchen in Seesen, Germany, 1850, 124 years after Cristofori had perfected his piano in Italy.

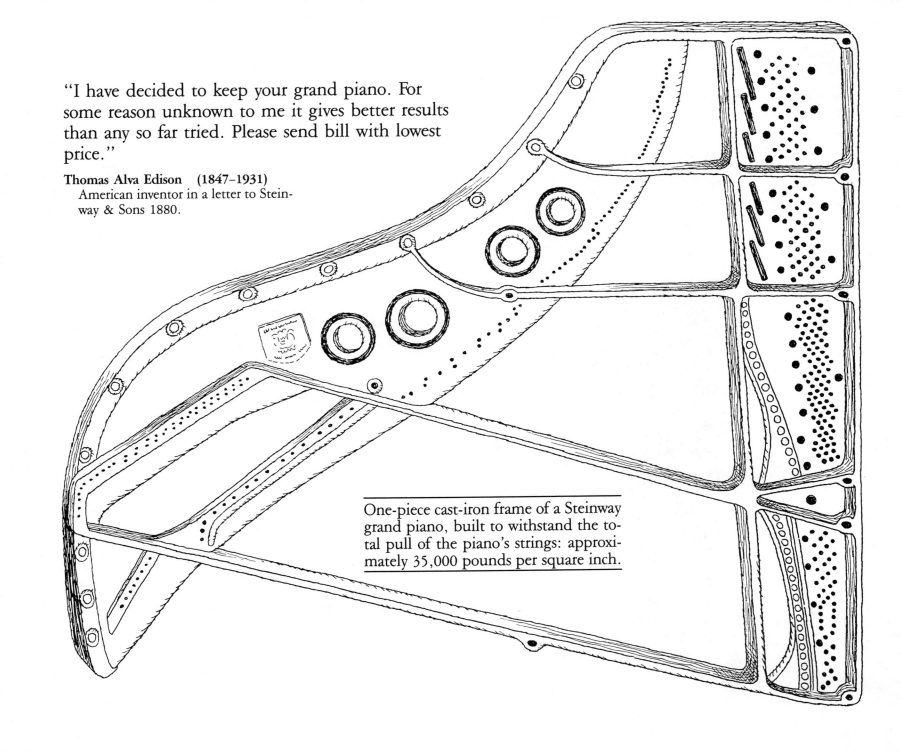

"I have decided to keep your grand piano. For some reason unknown to me it gives better results than any so far tried. Please send bill with lowest price."

Thomas Alva Edison (1847–1931)
American inventor in a letter to Steinway & Sons 1880.

One-piece cast-iron frame of a Steinway grand piano, built to withstand the total pull of the piano's strings: approximately 35,000 pounds per square inch.

"There is one thing stronger
than all the armies in the world:
and that is an idea whose time has come."

Victor Marie Hugo   (1802–1885)
French poet and novelist.

Baby
Grand
Piano
R I M

A grand piano's wooden rim is a laminated plank of 22 hard-maple slats, each 12 inches wide and 3/16th–inch thick. Wood of same growth, grade, texture are glued together — side-by-side, back-to-back. While the glue is still wet, this plank is bent around a monster steel form by manpower to be held firmly by clamps. Now two wide copper strips hug the rim, front and back, while a high-frequency generator sets up a magnetic field between them that dries the glue in seven minutes. After that not even opposing teams of draft horses could pull the strips apart. — *B.B.*

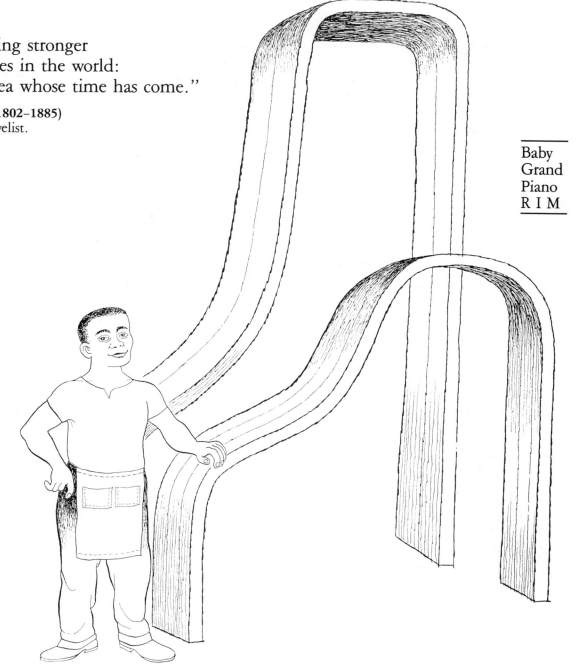

"The multitude, who require to be led, still hate their masters."

William Hazlitt (1778–1830)
British literary critic and essayist.
Characteristics

Delivery of a
concert grand
Nagpur, India,
circa 1923

"Women always excel men in that sort of wisdom which comes from experience. To be a woman is in itself a terrible experience."

Henry Louis Mencken   **(1880–1956)**
American journalist, critic, and philologist.
Masculum et Feminam Creavit Eos 1920

"Music needs air, sunlight, and liberty to be alive. It is only then that it will impart to us surprising secrets."

Wanda Landowska   **(1877–1959)**
Polish concert pianist, harpsichord virtuoso
Landowska on Music 1964.

"The piano is the most massive of the devices by which the young are tortured in the name of education and the grownup in the name of entertainment."

Arthur Loesser   **(1894–1969)**
American composer.

Preface to *Men, Women, and Pianos* 1954

"Through the window the edges of the forest were in sight, waiting to close in on the clearing again, throwing out small shrub, tendril, and vine across the path, waiting for another year, another century. Persistently, against the shrieking of the jungle birds, rose the sound of a melodeon in the schoolroom, the blending sweetness of the children's voices. They were singing 'Swing Low Sweet Chariot', translated into Kiswahili."

John Latouche
American poet, journalist, satirist, playwright (anti-imperialist theatricals), television director, U.S. Navy Seabee.

John Latouche/photos by Andre Cauvin *Congo* 1945

Master Piano Builders

Henry Z. Steinway, looking back on age 70, fourth-generation member of that illustrious family of piano makers, cannot play the instrument. "I'm not musical," he says. "It's a hand, eye, ear coordination you have to learn." Henry estimates 95 percent of concert pianists play Steinways: Horowitz (since 1925), Rubinstein, Serkin, Ashkenazy, Elton John, plus about 500 other staunch loyalists. The Steinways, contrary to popular belief, did not invent the piano. The first idea for hammer action to strings came to a now-nameless Dutchman in 1610, and 88 years later, in 1698, Cristofori began to build keyboard instruments that would "speak like the heart with the delicate touch of an angel." By 1726 he put all the essentials of a modern piano into his new keyboard instrument, a curiosity shunned by most contemporary musicians who saw no need for anything louder than their chamber-concert instruments. In 1740, Gottfried Silbermann began building pianofortes for the Prussian king Frederick the Great — 15 by 1747. Square pianos came from harpsichord makers: Zumpe, Hildebrand, Tschudin, Broadwood. The piano's first public appearance in a concert was in 1768 — a Zumpe square played by Bach's youngest son, Johann Christian. The giant of early piano makers, Johann Andreas Stein, of Augsburg (1728–1792), was trained by Silbermann. The first piano in France by Sebastian Érard. His ad was on a handbill announcing Liszt's Parisian debut as a prodigy, aged twelve. The first upright was built in 1800 by John Isaac Hawkins. The spinet was introduced in 1811 by Robert Wornum. The Steinways repotted their roots in America two years after the German revolution of 1848, when a son, Carl, emigrated here, got work as a cabinetmaker, and soon sent for the rest of his clan: father, mother, three sisters, three brothers. A fourth, Theodor, didn't come over until 1865, twelve years after the others had left their jobs in various piano factories to combine in forming their own company, which, in 1972, after 107 years of successful operation, was sold to the Columbia Broadcasting System, ". . . assuring the continuity of the Steinway piano," Henry says. The sale also gave Steinway stockholders a harmonious trade of their holdings for CBS securities. The company builds about 4,000 pianos a year, two percent of the 200,000 made annually in America. The Price of a Steinway ranges from $5,900 for a 40″ "little vertical," dubbed the Contemporary, to $39,000 and up for a 9′ ebony concert grand. — *B.B.*

"Wagner's music is better than it sounds."

Mark Twain (1835–1910)
American humorist, lecturer, travel writer,
novelist.
Real name: Samuel Langhorne Clemens

"You round the back of
your throat and throw the
column of air into vibration
without forcing it out: and
when you want to make a
crescendo . . . you pull down
your diaphragm, arch your
soft palate, and enlarge
the instrument generally,
but you don't blow . . ."

George Bernard Shaw   (1856–1950)
  in a letter to the musician Arnold
  Dolmetsch, regarding the production
  of vocal tone from *Collected Letters
  1911–1925* edited by
  Dan H. Lawrence (1985.)

"If I had the power I would insist on
all oratorios being sung in the costume
of the period — with a possible
exception of *The Creation*."

Sir Ernest Newman
English journalist.

The *New York Post* 1924

"I like Wagner's music better than anybody's.
It's so loud that no one can talk the whole time
without other people hearing what one says."

Oscar Wilde   (1854–1900)
  The Picture of Dorian Grey 1891.

"The Most High has a decided taste
for vocal music, provided it be
lugubrious and gloomy enough."

François Marie Arouet de Voltaire   (1694–1778)
  French historian, essayist, politi-
  cal activist, and patron of theatrical performers.

  Dictionnaire philosophique, 1751

"Bach is
the foundation
of piano playing,
Liszt the summit.
The two make
Beethoven possible."

**Ferruccio Busoni
(1866–1924)**
*Rules for
Practicing
the Piano*
1898

Johann Sebastian Bach   (1685–1750)

From an engraving
of the period

"Bach opens a vista to the universe.
After experiencing him, people feel there
is meaning to life after all."

Helmut Walcha   (1907–   )
Blind German organist

Dr. Laurence J. Peter
Peter's Quotations 1977.

"Like three eternally recurring cards in the musical deck, Bach, Beethoven, and Mozart are dealt out with a monotonous regularity that enrages a Handel or Wagner cultist. However, there can be no doubt that a vote taken today would favor Johann Sebastian Bach for first, or, just possibly, second place."

Wallace Brockway and Herbert Weinstock
Men of Music 1950

"Whether the angels play only Bach praising God, I am not quite sure; I am sure, however, that *en famille* they play Mozart."

Karl Barth   (1886–1968)
Swiss theologian, led the German Protestant Church in opposition to Hitler and the Nazis, 1935.

An obituary quote
The New York Times 11 December 1968

"Medicine, to produce health, must know disease; music, to produce harmony, must know discord."

Plutarch (ca 46 AD–120 AD)
Greek philosopher, essayist, biographer.

A grand salaam to *The New Yorker*'s Eustice Tilley, his perennial monocle and butterfly. Readers were uplifted by a recent leadoff to *The Talk Of The Town* regarding the 1986 nuclear arms talks in Geneva, and their odd relation to the music of Bach. The thought was advanced that the attendant politicos who would be speaking of "megatons, verification, throw-weight, and the like" might, at some point, let "some strains of the music of Bach" seep into the proceedings, in hope that the music will remind negotiators "as it has reminded all of us, why they must succeed." Amen. — *B.B.*

"I write music as a sow piddles."

Wolfgang Amadeus Mozart (1756–1791)

Baptized:
Johannes Chrysostomus
Wolfgangus Theophilus

Austrian composer, keyboard player, violist, violinist, orchestra conductor

From an engraving of the period

Amadeus is Latin for "love of God," as is Gottlieb in German, and Theophilus in Greek. The fierceness of the name Wolfgangus rings strangely among all that God-love, especially as it stands next to Chrysostomus which, in Greek, relates to golden-mouthed. Also, in childhood Mozart was affectionately called Wolferl, and his wife's pet name for him was Wolfie.

"Never did Mozart write for eternity, and it is for precisely that reason that much of what he wrote is for eternity."

Albert Einstein (1879–1955)
U.S. theoretical physicist; formulation theory of relativity.

"He took musical small change of his day learned from childhood, and transformed it into a mint of gold."

Michael Kennedy (1926–   )
Musical savant, journalist, editor, author.
Speaking of Mozart:
The Concise Oxford Dictionary of Music 1980

"If only the whole world could feel the power of harmony."
Wolfgang Amadeus Mozart

Wolfgang Amadeus Mozart

"A most intense young man,
A soulful-eyed young man,
An ultra-poetical, super-aesthetical,
Out-of-the-way young man!"

**Sir William Schwenk
Gilbert   (1836–1911)**
  English playwright, humorist, and for over 20 years,
  comic-opera collaborator
  with Sir Arthur Sullivan.

  Patience 1881

From an engraving of the period

Ludwig van
Beethoven as a
young man.

"Life is but thought: so think I will
That youth and I are house-mates still."

Samuel Taylor Coleridge   (1772–1834)
  English poet, critic, and philosopher

  Youth and Age

"Everybody's youth is a dream,
a form of chemical madness."

Francis Scott Key Fitzgerald   (1896–1940)
  American short-story writer,
  novelist.

  *The Diamond as Big as the
  Ritz*

"Why should a man, whose blood is warm within,
Sit like his grandsire cut in alabaster?"

William Shakespeare
  English poet, player, and playwright.

The Merchant of Venice I.i. 1596

Beethoven as
an old man
(1770–1827)

"Nothing is less worthy of honor than an old man who has no other evidence of having lived long except his age."

Lucius Annaeus Seneca (ca 4 B.C.–A.D. **65**)
Roman statesman and philosopher.

De tranquillitate animi A.D. 62–63

"In the white light, dwarfed in the massive space, the reason for dreaming and playing is made clear. We are such small, timorous souls with such gargantuan appetites. What is there for us but the imagined strength and comforting evasion of myth?"

John Lahr (1941–   )
American theatrical essayist, critic.
A critique of *Orlando Furioso* performed in Italian, NYC, *Teatro Libero di Roma.*

Astonish Me: essays on the NYC theater 1973.

"Every man desires to live long, but no man would be old."

Jonathan Swift
British satirist.

Thoughts on Various Subjects 1713

Beethoven, born in Bonn, died in Vienna, age 57.

Ludwig van Beethoven

"I occasionally play works by contemporary
composers and for two reasons.
First to discourage the composer
from writing any more
and secondly to remind myself
how much I appreciate Beethoven."

Jascha Heifetz (1901–   )
Concert violinist
Lithuanian-born; American citizen 1925.

Life magazine: 28 July 1961

"When you do that, Cab, and
when you get to Beethoven's Fifth,
you goin' to give it an upbeat
or a downbeat? Tell me that!"

Thomas "Fats" Waller (1904–1943)
American composer, singer, and
master of stride piano.

Response to Cab Calloway
when he boasted that one
day he would be leading
a symphonic orchestra.

Ain't Misbehavin' 1975 Ed Kirkeby
in collaboration with
Duncan P. Schledt, Sinclair Traill

From an engraving of the period

Franz Peter Schubert

(1797–1828)

Schubert dearly loved to play four-handed piano.

"Two souls with but a single thought,
Two hearts that beat as one."

Friedrich Halm   **(1806–1871)**
Austrian dramatist, poet.
Pseudonym of: Eligius Franz Joseph
Von Münch-Bellinghausen

Schubert, born in Himmelfortgrund, a suburb of Vienna, was one of fifteen children. Only five survived infancy. He is considered the world's greatest composer of love songs — more than 600, not counting concert arias. Though it was said that "he could set a hand-bill to music," he wrote serious music for 70 poems by Goethe, 60 by Schiller.

"People who make music together cannot be enemies, at least not while the music lasts."

Paul Hindemith   **(1895–1963)**
German-American composer, violist.

Franz Peter Schubert

"Everything he touches turns to music."

Robert Alexander Schumann   **(1810–1856)**
   German romantic composer
   In praise of Franz Schubert.

"Composers should write tunes
that chauffeurs and errand boys
can whistle."

Sir Thomas Beecham
   British symphonic conductor.

"A tune is always the same tune,
whether it is sung loudly or softly,
by a child or a man, whether it is
played on a flute or on a trombone."

Charles Robert Darwin   **(1809–1882)**
   British naturalist, author
   *The Expressions of the Emotions
   in Man and Animals*

From an engraving of the period

"Composing is one thing
performing's another,
listening's a third.
What can they have
to do with one another?"

John Cage   **(1912–   )**
   American sonic composer.

Twentieth Century Music
Peter Yates 1967

After an etching
by Ingres

"Beethoven and Liszt have contributed
to the advent of long hair."

**Louis Moreau Gottschalk
(1829–1869)**
American pianist, com-
poser, conductor.

Ferencz (Franz) Liszt

A pianist of dazzling splendor. His musical idol, the
flamboyant Paganini. Liszt, dreamily handsome Hungarian,
the first stage artist to play a "concert" alone, first to play a
concert piano in profile. As a feckless young man, he toured
Europe, from Portugal to Turkey, in a horse-drawn gypsy
caravan: salon by day, boudoir by night. An earthy man all
his life, with 26 major love affairs — one with Lola Montez,
several fetching illegitimates. He was enchanted with the
occult and necromancy, enjoyed basking in the high-rise
titillation of Mephistophelian charm. A mountebank who
loved to conjure up demonic worlds in which to play
four-handed with the devil, searing keyboards with hot
satanic ashes.

"It got to a point where
I had to get a haircut
or a violin."

Franklin Delano Roosevelt (1882–1945)
31st President, The United States.

Readers Digest, May 1938

Liszt's
Cloven-
Hoofers

———————

Faust Symphony
Malediction
Totentanz
Two Episodes
from Lenaus Faust
Mephisto Waltzes
Nocturnal Procession
The Dance in the
Village Inn
(first *Mephisto*
waltz)

"Why should the Devil
have all the good tunes?"

Attributed to John Calvin   (1509–1564)

"The Devil was sick:
The Devil a monk would be;
The Devil was well:
The Devil a monk was he."

Old English rhyme, traced in its
Latin form to 1450. Found in François Rabelais, *Works* IV. xxiv.

"Talk of the Devil and he'll appear."

Desiderius Erasmus (1466–1536)
Renaissance theologian.

"He needs must go that the devil drives"

An English proverb, first known in the 1560s, about forty years before it was used in Shakespeare's *All's Well That Ends Well* (I.iii) as "needs must when the Devil drives."

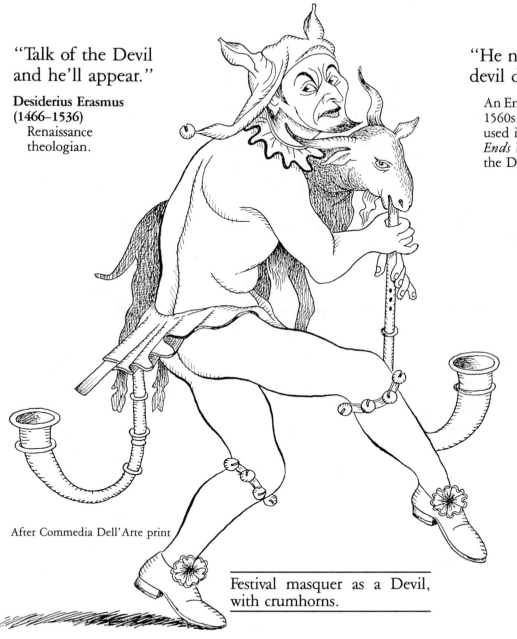

After Commedia Dell'Arte print

Festival masquer as a Devil, with crumhorns.

"The Devil as a roaring lion, walketh about, seeking whom he may devour."

The Holy Bible: I Peter, 5:8

"An apology for the Devil — it must be remembered that we have only heard one side of the case. God has written all the books."

Samuel Butler (1835–1902)
English journalist, author, painter, authority on the evolution of Homeric mythology.

"Over the piano was printed a notice:
'Please do not shoot the pianist.
He is doing his best.' "

Oscar Fingall O'Flahertie Wills Wilde
(aka: Sebastian Melmoth, after
his release from imprisonment
in 1895 for "immoral conduct"
concerning Lord Alfred Douglas,
young son of the marquess of
Queensbury.)

English author, poet, journalist

Report an 1882
lecture tour of
America's "wild West".

Impressions of America 1883

James Thurber   (1894–1961)
American humorist, artist.

The World of John McNulty, 1946

"It's a pity to shoot the pianist when the piano is out of tune."

Rene Coty   (1882–1962)
President of France, 4th Republic, 1954.

Time magazine 4 Jan. 1957

"McNulty and I were reporters together on Columbus, Ohio, newspapers in the early nineteen-twenties. He did general assignments for a morning paper while I covered City Hall for an afternoon paper, but our offices were just a few blocks apart, in the center of town, and I bunked into him almost every day, often at the corner of Broad and High streets, the city's main intersection. He was invariably excited about something, the cabin lights of the Shenandoah which he had seen twinkling in the sky the night before, a girl at the James Theatre who sang 'Roses Are Shining in Picardy,' Donn Byrne's novel *The Changelings*, which he demanded that I begin reading right away, there on that crowded corner, or a song called 'Last Night on the Back Porch,' which he insisted on playing for me, then and almost there. Actually, he took me around the corner to a music store and began beating out the song on the first piano he came to, to the astonishment of the store's staff. 'It's McNulty,' I explained to them in a whisper and they all nodded and breathed his name in unison, obviously believing that he was a great pianist, come to play at Memorial Hall, who had suddenly been seized by a rare moment of relaxation and frivolity. He had once played the piano in a movie theatre in the days of silent films and, within his range, there wasn't anything he couldn't make the keys do. While playing 'My Gal Sal' he used to recite the succession to the presidency, and it was upon the conclusion of that bravura performance that we left the music shop and its startled and transfigured staff."

"Each honest calling, each walk of life, has its own elite, its own aristocracy based upon excellence of performance."

James Bryant Conant **(1893–1978)**
American organic chemist, educator
Harvard University President '33.

"There was a gentleman who rendered a selection at the piano, very marvelous music that made me want to play the piano very, very much. The only trouble was that this gentleman had long bushy hair, and because the piano was known in our circle as an instrument for a lady, this confirmed me in my idea that if I played piano I would be misunderstood."

Ferdinand "Jelly Roll" Morton   (1885–1941)
American master jazz pianist
(Real name: Ferdinand Joseph La Menthe).

Hear Me Talkin' to Ya 1955
edited by Nat Hentoff and Nat Shapiro

"Jelly Roll" Morton

"If a guy's got it, let him give it. I'm selling music, not prejudice."

Benny Goodman   (1909–1986)
American jazz clarinetist, first orchestra conductor to integrate blacks into a big-time jazz band.

The Saturday Evening Post
18 December 1954

"Jelly Roll" Morton   He Kept On Rollin'

Ferdinand Joseph La Menthe, born late September 1885, Storyville, New Orleans tenderloin district. His boyhood was nose-in-dirt struggle. No wonder that he stammered. Pool shark, nostrums peddler, confidence man, card sharp, freelance hustler at bawdy houses. Then they were luxuriant palaces of pleasure, not held in disdain. their "blue book" clients' guidebook described parlor furnishings much more opulent than those of the city's private mansions listed in tourist guides. Dance bands then had no pianists. Key ticklers made a lot more money working bars and bordellos.

"Of course you wonder how the name Morton came by — it being an English name. I changed it when I started traveling. It is the name of my mother's second husband." Ferdinand didn't want to be called Frenchy, the label given to anyone with a Gallic name. Also, Frenchy carried a degrading sexual connotation. So, in fact, does "jelly roll."

Ferdinand became known as "the piano roll" and then just "the roll" because he played so tirelessly. His first piano composition was "Frog-i-more," written for a vaudeville contortionist named Moore. Then came "Trick Ain't Walkin' No More," a streetwalker's complaint. In Chicago, his "Jelly Roll Blues" set him on a patchy and wild musical career.

He added guitar and trombone to his piano prowess and toured Mississippi River-bottoms country with McCabes Minstrel Troubadours, followed by extended gigs in St. Louis and Chicago, hoppings about to San Francisco, Detroit, Cheyenne, Denver, Tia Juana, San Diego, and far-off Vancouver, B.C., and Alaska. For a time, he was a half-assed boxing promoter. He played MCA tours with various bands, and was at Roseland dancehall in New York for the lazy summer of 1928. In the fall he took his own band on tour, into 1930, when his cosmetic business failed. In '31, Harlem clubs; '36, Washington, D.C. at the Jungle Club, and in '38 he recorded his peregrinations for future generations, with Alan Lomax at the Library of Congress. He will be long remembered, this modern minstrel man who dreamed up and played and sang some of the lustiest laments ever heard about life on the dark side: scary, sexy ballads about drinking, doping, loving, disillusion, and disappointment. Frenchy La Menthe had come a long way from Storyville.

Jelly Roll Morton died in the Los Angeles County General Hospital in 1941, at age 56. "Morton gave the American dream an awful pummeling before it finally cut him down" was a comment of noted jazz buff and critic, Whitney Balliett. — B.B.

1857–1937

Julie Rivé-King

A champion concert pianist of the instrument's burgeoning days. Gave 400 solo recitals and starred with symphony orchestras more than 500 times. Had enormous endurance, fabulous memory. Once did 12 recitals in two weeks with no repeats.

"One hair of a woman can draw more than a hundred pair of oxen."

James Howell (ca. 1594–1666)
English author, born Carmarthenshire, S. Wales.

Familiar Letters 1621

"Music and women I cannot but give way to, whatever my business is."

Samuel Pepys (1633–1703)
English diarist and public servant, a benefactor of musicians.

Diary 9 March 1666.

"Music hath charms to soothe a savage breast,* To soften knotted oak."

William Congreve (1670–1729)
English dramatist, specialist in comedy.

The Mourning Bride I.i. 1697

* widely misquoted as "beast"

"We are the music-makers.
And we are the dreamers of dreams,
Wandering by lone sea-breakers,
And sitting by desolate streams;
World-losers and world-forsakers,
On whom the pale moon gleams:
Yet we are the movers and shakers
Of the world for ever, it seems."

Arthur William Edgar O'Shaughnessy **(1844–1880)**
English poet, specialist in ichthyology.

Epic of Women 1870

"Women indeed are the music of life; they absorb
everything more openly and unconditionally, in
order to embellish it by means of their sympathy."

Richard Wilhelm Wagner **(1813–1883)**
German dramatic composer, poet, essayist.
Letter to Theodor Uhlig, 27 Dec. 1849

Teresa Carreño

Eminent Venezuelan pianist, opera star, and
conductor. She played a command
performance for President Lincoln at the
White House. Told him the piano was out
of tune and improvised on his favorite
piece, "Listen to the Mocking Bird."

"There was an old man and he had a cow,
But he had no fodder to give her,
So he took up his fiddle, and played her a tune,
'Consider, good cow, consider;
This isn't the time for the grass to grow:
Consider, good cow, consider' "

Old folk tale, 250 years old. Farmer
explained to his cow that he had
nothing to feed her, that it was not
the growing season. He begged her
to be reasonable and considerate.
But the cow was not, and selfishly
died of hunger.

"The cow is of the bovine ilk;
One end is moo, the other milk."

Ogden Nash   (1902–1971)
American humorist,
verse maker.

"Whatsoever thy hand findeth to do,
do it with thy might."

Ecclesiastes 9:10
The favorite Biblical quote of the
father of Clarence Day, author of
Life With Father 1935.

Vladimir de Pachmann

Vladimir de Pachmann (1848–1933): keyboard clown of
the concert circuit. During recitals he made comical faces,
muttered, and lectured his audiences. He idolized
Chopin but did not play him superbly. Some critics
dubbed de Pachmann "The Chopinzee." Backstage he
wore an aged tattered bathrobe, claimed to have be-
longed to Chopin. When it wore out another, also credited to Chopin, would take its place.

"Pale hands I loved beside the Shalimar,
Where are you now? Who lies beneath your spell?
. . . I would have rather felt you round my throat,
Crushing our life, than waving me farewell."

Adela Nicolson ("Laurence Hope")
Kashmiri Song

"The cat is in the parlor,
the dog is in the lake;
The cow is in the hammock —
what difference does it make?"

Anonymous childhood
chant ca. 1910

"Every one as they like,
as the woman said
when she kissed her cow."

Pierre Antoine Motteux (1663–1718)
French translator, dramatist,
English-Scottish interpolation
in translation of Rabelais
V. xxix. 1693.

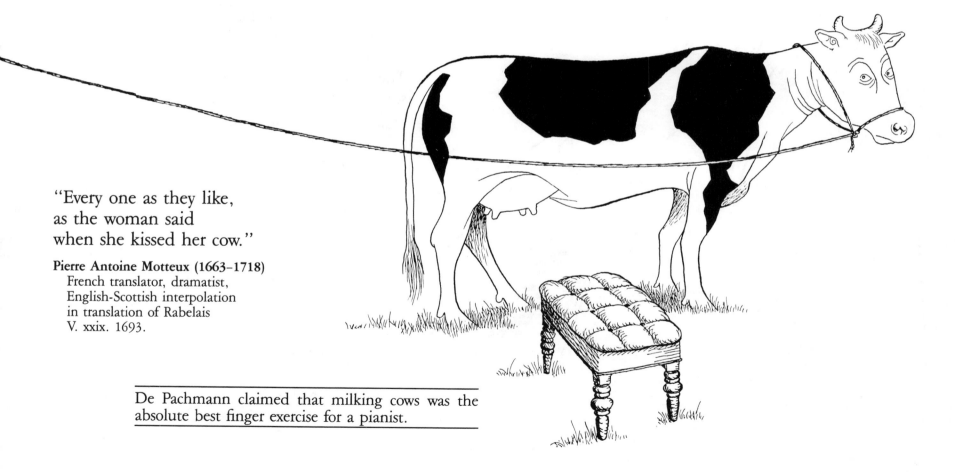

De Pachmann claimed that milking cows was the
absolute best finger exercise for a pianist.

"Piano playing is more difficult than statesmanship.
It is harder to wake emotions in ivory keys than
it is in human beings."

Ignacy Jan Paderewski **(1860–1941)**
Polish pianist, composer, statesman

"The attraction of the virtuoso
for the public is very like that
of the circus for the crowd.
There is always the hope that
something dangerous will happen."

Claude Achille Debussy **(1862–1918)**
French composer

Monsieur Croche, Anti-Dilletante
a book of music criticism.
In French, *croche* is the
eighth note or quaver.

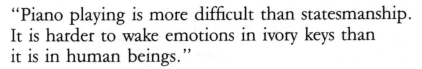

Vladimir Horowitz

Vladimir Horowitz

Born Volodya Gorovitz, Kiev, Russia. Father, Samuel (aka Simeon); mother, Sophie. Youngest of four, all musically avid. At 21, Vladimir left his homeland and in two years made his American debut as soloist with the New York Philharmonic, Sir Thomas Beecham conducting. Critics raved: "amazing strength, dazzling technique, irresistable youth and temperament." Horowitz was off and running. In 1933 he met and married Wanda Toscanini, aged 26 — an often stormy union. Horowitz is considered the greatest showman of concert pianists. Effortless playing: elegant, probing, capricious, introspective, artless, spontaneous, and excitingly heroic — a notable survivor of modern piano virtuosi, in the mold of Liszt. Touring was hard on Vladimir. Off the road: 1936–'38, '53–'65, '67–'74. Public appearances, 1983 fell below his high standards. With renewed vigor, at age 81, a comeback tour took him to five European cities (plenty shekels) and a home-life-documentary film and tv rights will add to his *gonfiato* bank account.

Drawn from a photo in TIME magazine credited to *Musical America Magazine*

A roguish Vladimir, the life of a *bon voyage* party, circa 1926, with musical friends: Nathan Milstein, Gregor Piatigorsky, Arturo Toscanini (later to be Vladimir's father-in-law), and Bernardino Molinari.

"The man who, as so often happens, chose the path of art because he was aware of his difference, soon learns that he can nourish his art and his difference solely by his resemblance to all."

Albert Camus   **(1913–1960)**
French novelist, journalist, existentialist.
Nobel Prize acceptance speech 1957.

VLADIMIR and WANDA
Encounter the Stunks

Excerpted
from a report
by TIME magazine
correspondent,
Dean Brelis . . .
5 May 1986

Vladimir Horowitz, a sartorial super-snapper octogenarian, in a dark blue oxford suit, blue-and-white bow tie and a black Borsalino, sits in a VIP NYC airport lounge, awaiting a flight to Washington, D.C. Wanda, his wife for 53 years, who dislikes bureaucratic functions, is a trifle testy. "I hope Mrs. Reagan will be there," she says. Horowitz trusts that the pilot won't land in the Potomac. "I forgot my galoshes." Wanda retorts, "That's not funny." But the plane lands okay and when the all-clear bell sounds Vladimir notes, "F sharp." Wanda again hopes that Mrs. Reagan will be there. The USIA rep who meets the couple at the gate says otherwise — only the President will be present. "I am insulted," says Wanda and backs off on going to the White House. "She's temperamental," explains Horowitz. "Toscanini*, you know." Then the limo is not permitted to use the taxi lane. "That does it," snaps Wanda. "I will go back to New York." Vladimir quickly agrees. "If she's not going, then I'm not going." Panic, then a compromise: the distinguished guests take a taxi. At the drab security check Wanda again bristles. "Is there a mistake?" On a previous visit they'd entered through the impressive front-door pillars. "Now they bring us to the servants' entrance," Wanda sniffs. "You can send me back to New York immediately." Instead, the noble pair are hustled into the Oval Office to meet our nation's Chief Executive and to be subjected to a grand-scale "photo opportunity." Back in Manhattan Wanda continues to fume. Her celebrated father once told her that government functions are very bad theatre and that too many people in government are stunks. *Stunks?* "Short for stinkers," explains Wanda.

* Wanda is Toscanini's daughter.

Horowitz quotes are from a *New York Times* interview by Will Crutchfield

"I am like Schubert.

I do not make music for the money.

Schubert once sent money back to a publisher, because he thought the piece was not a good piece. I like that."

Has Mr. Horowitz ever sent back a check after a recital, an interviewer asked. Vladimir giggled, responded, "Never." And got a wry look from his wife.

Horowitz's recent concert tour to five European cities (Moscow, Leningrad, Hamburg, Berlin, and London) grossed two-and-a-half million dollars.

"The piano is a singing instrument. Sing, sing, sing at the piano."

His advice to Byron Janis, a 15-year-old prodigy student.

"I am not tired of life. I can still feel wonder when it is a beautiful day."

"I married an angel. She married a devil. There was a devil in me then."

"Beethoven is sometimes boring. For example, the *Missa Solemnis*. I prefer Lehar."

"I did not have to develop a technique. It was there from the beginning."

"I have never forgotten my Russia. I remember the smells when the snow melts and the spring arrives."

"I had to go back to Russia before I died. It brings an Aristotelian unity to my life, like a coda in music."

"I think that long after the people have forgotten who won the Tchaikovsky competition they will remember that an American won it. This is important."

Van Cliburn (1934–   )
  American concert pianist
  Winner of the 1958
  International Piano Festival,
  Moscow, U.S.S.R.

"Whoe'er excells
in what we prize,
Appears a hero
in our eyes."

Jonathan Swift (1667–1745)
  Dean of St. Patrick's,
  Dublin, British satirist.

  Cadenus and Vanessa, a poetic effort
  to soothe a persistent lover whose ad-
  vances had been rejected for 33 years.
  1723

Thick curly blond hair, wondrous blue eyes, six-feet, four inches tall, long strong fingers that span ten notes with ease, a man noted for his warmth and friendliness.

Van Cliburn

Van Cliburn (signature)

Champion of Musical Youth

Harvey Lavan Cliburn, Jr., born Shreveport, La. Mother, concert pianist, teacher. Father, an oil tycoon. Van began piano lessons at three, played in public at six. At 20 he'd already won five major U.S. piano competitions, had played Carnegie Hall with New York Philharmonic. In 1958, he was sent to first international Tchaikovsky competition in Moscow. His performances sold out during one of the city's worst winter storms. Won first prize: gold medal and 25,000 rubles ($2,500). He'd arrived in Russia with three suitcases, went home with 17, plus a lilac bush to be planted on Rachmaninoff's grave in N.Y. at Valhalla. New York City went mad over Van: Broadway ticker-tape parade; four concerts with the Philharmonic; RCA recording contract; national TV; home-coming concert at Carnegie Hall. Abram Chasins, oracle of radio WQXR, scorned the hysteria: "The Russians didn't discover Van Cliburn. What their people value, ours ignore. No one paid attention to Van when he won all those exacting U.S. competitions." Van took the hubbub gracefully. "I'm not a success, I'm a sensation. Success is a very difficult term to use, especially about yourself." Van Cliburn gave up performing, 1978, at age 44. Called it a sabbatical. Friends urged him to announce retirement. His response: "What if you have to call up your manager three months later to say, 'I'm starving'? Clearly, he is not. Van contributed $50,000 to the 1985 Van Cliburn International Piano Competition.

"Competitions are for horses, not artists."

Béla Bartók   (1881–1945)
   Hungarian composer, pianist.
   b. Nagyszentmiklós, Transylvania.

   appeared in *Saturday Review* 25 August 1962

"You cannot know how it spoils one to have been a child prodigy."

Ferencz (Franz) Liszt   (1811–1886)
   Hungarian composer, concert
   pianist
   A child prodigy

Artur Rubinstein

"Artur Rubinstein was at my house last night.
He is a very cute guy, around sixty,
and still likes to look the frails over.
But he wouldn't play the piano for me."

Julius (Groucho) Marx
Life With Groucho
Arthur Marx 1954

"Please don't tell Mr. Hurok, but I love playing the
piano so much that I would do it for nothing."

Artur Rubinstein (1887–1982)
Polish-born concert pianist virtuoso
American citizen 1946.

Rubinstein Speaking
- N.Y. *Times* Sunday Magazine 26 Jan. 1964

". . . sometimes when I sit down
to practice and there is no one else in
the room I have to stifle my impulse
to ring for the elevator man and
offer him money to come in
and hear me."

Artur Rubinstein *Holiday* magazine May 1963

A Rubinstein Concerto

Excerpted from "This Ageless Hero Rubinstein" by Donal Henahan. The New York *Times* Magazine 1976

Rubinstein wasn't heavy (165) or tall (five-eight), but he was built half-acrobat (heavy chest and husky biceps) and half pole-vaulter (extra long legs). He felt he looked comical onstage. ". . . I mean it is rather ridiculous, because a fat little man like me to appear there in evening dress looks like an undertaker, you know funeral things and the piano has a little look of a coffin, if you like to know."

Rubinstein once tried to hang himself — at age 21 in Berlin. His career was on the fritz, he was flat broke, he'd run up hotel and restaurant bills he couldn't pay, and he'd been unable to get concert dates. He tried to do the deed in the bathroom with his bathrobe belt. It broke and he was a foolish heap on the floor. "If I saw today such a scene on television," he writes in his memoirs, "I would roar with laughter."

Rubinstein's six brothers and sisters disappeared along with six million other Jews during World War II.

Rubinstein escaped most ills of the elderly: no rheumatic aches, no arthritis, no stiff joints. Pills? Only Vitamin C, swore by it. Enjoyed the finest wines, the most expensive cigars (two, three daily, always with coffee). He arose no later than 8, did 20 minutes of stretches before a hearty breakfast.

Rubinstein, nearing 90, recorded five Beethoven concertos in seven-and-a-half sessions, a total of just under 19 hours. That would have exhausted even a young man.

Rubinstein, 7th-born, 1887. Father, aged 40. Arthur died 1982, age 95. That is 91 years after he'd first touched piano keys, and 76 after his Carnegie Hall debut, age 19. A survivor.

Rubinstein, at a meeting in Jerusalem with a Nobel Prize winner, S.Y. Agron: "I said to him, 'Do you like music?'. And he said, 'I don't know. This is the first time in my life that I go to a concert. But I *like* how you sit so straight at the piano.'

Rubinstein was a lively agnostic. "When I was a child, I looked and I did not see any god. I doubt if Moses saw him, really. All those little girls who saw the Virgin. All that, no, a lie. They did not convince me. Jeanne d'Arc, charming story, but not my idea of what is. Arabs and Israelis, what do they want of each other? The Arabs have Mohammed, Israel has another fellow, so they say, sorry, but we must kill you for that. So, long ago, I decided I did not see any god. We are put here on this earth without being asked."

Rubinstein had the largest hands ever to grace a concert pianist. He could span an octave, plus four more keys.

a Rubinstein Encore

". . . the public fills the hall, let's say. They come after a good dinner. The women look at each other or at other women's dresses. Men think mostly about business or some games or some sports or God knows what. And there I have this crowd not entirely quite musical, not really knowers of music, but who like music, who love music.

"And that is a very difficult proposition. I have to hold them, you know, in attention, by my emotion — nothing else. I can't look at them, I can't make faces, I can't tell them now comes a great moment, now you listen, now is a great thing for you — nothing of the kind. I have to play. Look there, straight in front of me. But there is a certain antenna: There is a certain secret thing which goes out, emanates from me, from my emotion, from the feeling, you like to call it 'soul' if you like to.

"I don't know what 'soul' means, but it is a word which one uses very much without knowing what it represents really. But this something which, let me call it for the moment 'soul' if you like, projects something which I do feel. I do feel that it is doing it. It suddenly puts the audience into my hands. There is a moment where I feel them all here. I can do anything. I can

hold them as one little note in the air. They will not breathe because they wait what happens next, you know, what will come in the music. That is a great, great moment. Not always does it happen, but when it does happen it is a great moment of our lives.

"Well, I must say, I always had a sensual, not sensuous, feeling of my fingers when I had to strike something which goes out of my inner self. When I have to sing out the nocturne of Chopin, I sing it inside. But I sing it like a love song, you see. And then, under my fingers I feel it . . . what you said, I feel a rather sensual pleasure, you know, in touching it. I become excited when I touch an E-flat which will give that sound which I need to hear."

from "Rubinstein,"
an interview with
Robert McNeil
"Rubinstein at 90"
WNET Channel 13 1977

"**Fats**"
Waller

"... bestial cries ... neighing horses, the squeal of a brass pig, crying jackasses, amorous quacks of an amorous toad ... excruciating medley of brutal sounds ... a barely perceptible rhythm ... screaming music ... an orchestra of madmen, sexual maniacs, led by a man-stallion beating with an enormous phallus."

Maxim Gorky (1868–1936)
Russian author, playwright
(Pen name of Alexy Maximovich Peshkov)
His description of an American jazz band.

"Ladies and gentlemen, I play the piano, but tonight *God* is in the house."

Thomas "Fats" Waller (1904–1943)
To a nightclub audience, in announcing that jazz-pianist virtuoso, Art Tatum, was in the house that evening.

Ain't Misbehavin' 1975 Ed Kirkeby
in collaboration with
Duncan Schledt, Sinclair Traill

Mister Stride Piano

In New York City's Harlem, at 107 West 134th Street, in early morning 21 May 1904, was born Thomas "Fats" Waller. His father, a trucker, was hoping to become a gospel preacher. Whenever that transpired, his wife planned to sing in the choir, play the piano and organ.

At age six, Thomas began pretending to play piano on the seats of lined-up chairs. Eventually, his mother and her half-brother pooled funds to buy an upright piano. But no lessons for Tommy until the twelfth and last baby was born. Then the growing boy blossomed. An elder brother's girlfriend took the kid to his first nickleodeon to see a cowboys-Indians thriller. He was enchanted — not by the capers being unreeled on the big screen, but by their piano accompaniment. "That's for me," said Thomas, who by now was called 'Fats.'

He had to wait a spell to get what he wanted. While waiting, he took a job in a lower Manhattan jewelry factory, buffing ring boxes. On weekends, as delivery boy for a neighborhood deli, using his plump innocence, he sneakily supplied select customers with bootleg hootch.

A kindly sexton of a neighborhood church let Fats practice piano there just before the afternoon services. Harlem then was jumping with lively theaters and speakeasies galore. Pianos tinkled and banged all night long in every other cellar along 133-34th streets, west of Lennox Avenue. All jive, and all alive!

Fats spent his off-time at Harlem's famous vaudeville theater, the Lincoln. He never knew what flickered across the movie screen, but he absorbed every mood and move of the in-house pianist, Mazie Mullins — then his idol. On a break she often let him spell her in the piano pit. Soon he was allowed to play interval music on the theater's pipe organ, just before the stage show went on. When Mazie became ill the boy wonder stepped into the breach and later (at $23 a week), Fats was hired to replace the Lincoln's regular organist who'd quit without notice. Fats soon developed his own jazzy way of playing, popular with audiences. His father was appalled by his son's working in "a house of Satan." Jazz was never accepted in the family.

Fats joined the modest dance band of a local drummer, and with it played small social engagements on weekends. Fats heard his first real jazz music played in a tent dancehall. There from James P. Johnson, King of the Keys, Fats soon learned jazz fundamentals. More jazz input came at citified country dances, imported in their original primitive form from down South, where they were all the rage. Fats truly was astounded. The music was made by harmonica, bone clappers, jaw harp, and jazz piano. Eventually, Fats took more formal lessons from a local Italian maestro.

In 1911 Fats met Jelly Roll Morton, married a longtime Harlemite friend, Edith Hackett, and plunged into vaudeville and the piano-roll trade. From then on, it was all golden gravy: nationwide tours, loved and lauded all over Europe, starred in Hollywood, a hit on Broadway, and countless recordings with famous jazz bands and on his own with his rowdy, blues-related stride piano and his raucous songs. He made hundreds of piano rolls and piled up thousands of bank rolls.

In 1943, Fats Waller was performing in Hollywood at the Florentine Gardens, in the Zanzibar Room, an after-hours spot, where a thousand guests could dine and dance with no sweat in the comfort of air conditioning. Unfortunately, blowers above and behind the Steinway grand poured a steady arctic blast on Fats' head and shoulders as he sat at the keyboard, dripping with perspiration. He never once complained. No one realized the danger. Fats caught the flu and was off ten days, with pneumonia. Then he came back to play out his contract — plus a series of wartime benefits and plenty of after-show partying, boozing, and playboying during the final week.

Fats barely and blearily made the early morning Sante Fe express to back east via Chicago. First day out of L.A. the train was buffeted by a gigantic Kansas-plains snowstorm so windy that Fats jokingly dubbed it a "Hawkins," after the blustery saxophone playing of his good friend Coleman Hawkins.

Alone in his stateroom, Fats died suddenly at about five a.m. A porter on his rounds discovered the death.

The train went on to Chicago where Fats' body was taken off for an autopsy. Oddly, during this emergency removal, his good friend, Louie Armstrong, was in another train sidetracked by the tragic event and awaiting clearance to move out. Told of the death by a pullman porter, Louie cried all the way to New York. — B.B.

olio

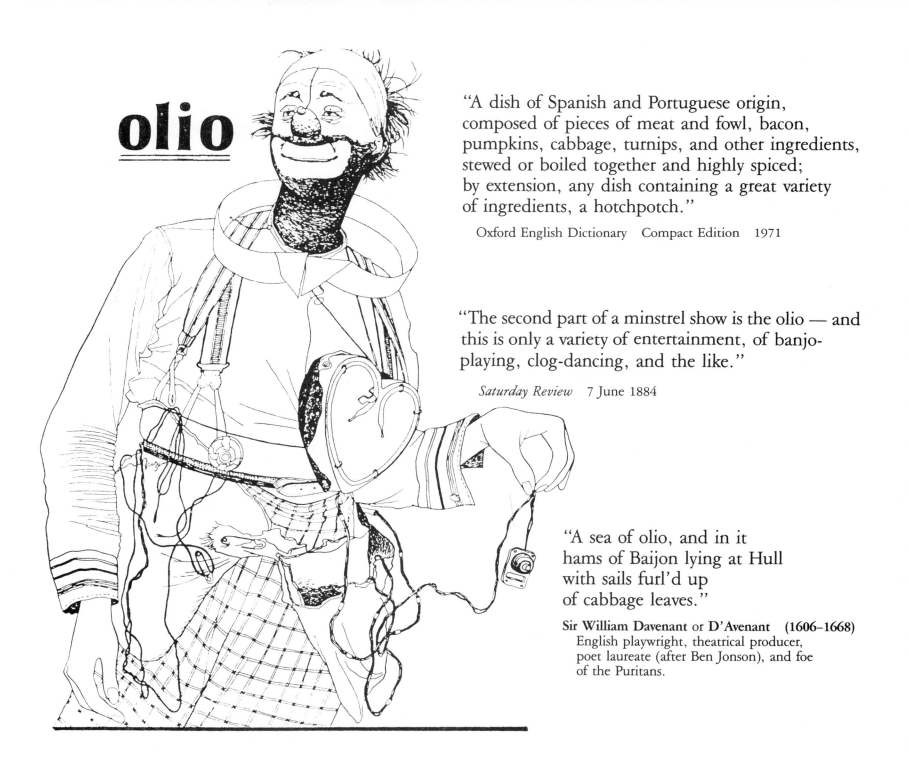

"A dish of Spanish and Portuguese origin, composed of pieces of meat and fowl, bacon, pumpkins, cabbage, turnips, and other ingredients, stewed or boiled together and highly spiced; by extension, any dish containing a great variety of ingredients, a hotchpotch."

Oxford English Dictionary   Compact Edition   1971

"The second part of a minstrel show is the olio — and this is only a variety of entertainment, of banjo-playing, clog-dancing, and the like."

Saturday Review   7 June 1884

"A sea of olio, and in it hams of Baijon lying at Hull with sails furl'd up of cabbage leaves."

Sir William Davenant or **D'Avenant**   **(1606–1668)**
English playwright, theatrical producer, poet laureate (after Ben Jonson), and foe of the Puritans.

Lou Jacobs

Lou Jacobs became
a circus man in 1924
at age 21. Now, 1986,
at age 83, he is the
star clown emeritus
of Ringling Bros. and
Barnum & Bailey Circus,
The Greatest Show
On Earth.

"I had rather have a fool to make me merry
than experience to make me sad."

William Shakespeare   (1564–1616)
English poet, player, playwright.

As You Like It IV.i. 1600

Lou's one-man-band (shown here circa 1948), a great sight gag,
but not his favorite musical instrument. His love is the musical
saw, played with a violin bow.

Lou's favorite music for it is the theme music of the film
Doctor Zhivago. It always was the feature of Lou's annual
musical-saw recital for the students of the Ringling Clown
College in the years that I was its director. Lou sat on the
arena's ring curb, bending saw held firmly between his knees,
and played along with a recording of that lugubrious
tear-nudger of frostbitten love. Each year we had to send out to
the record shops to find a new recording as Lou always
managed to mislay or lose the one we'd bought for him the
year previous. We were inclined to think that the once-a-year
onceover was all the lovelorn and snowbound doctor ever shared
with our distinguished sun-basking clown. — *B.B.*

"This fellow is wise enough to play the fool,
And to do that well craves a kind of wit."

William Shakespeare   (1564–1616)
Twelfth Night III,i. 1602

MUSICAL HAROLD

WIZARD OF MUSICAL GLASSES

"Time is a circus
always packing up
and moving away."

Ben Hecht (1894–1964)
American playwright.
Charlie, a tribute to
partner Charles McArthur

NOTES on the Origin of Musical Glasses

In 1677 a social observer noted "gay wine music" popular at parties, made by rubbing the rims of wine-filled glasses with moistened fingertips.

By the 1700s such foolery was formalized in Great Britain and Ireland. In 1743 Richard Pockrich began entertaining with a set of tuned glasses, an act continued for 16 years — until he burned to death in a music hall fire. In 1746 Christoph Willibald von Gluck gave two concerts for his patron Prince Lobkowitz, using "26 drinking glasses tuned with spring water." Other performers favored brandy, wine, beer, river, pump, and sea water. The Glass Harmonium was invented: shallow glass basins revolved by pedal through a trough of water. Ben Franklin made an adaptation which afforded full chords. That Harmonica made mystifying magical sound, described by a lyrical writer as ". . . a gentle virgin passing in the moonlight." — *B.B.*

Touches of Sweet Harmony

The Great Harold Smith

I first heard the musical glasses as a rookie circus clown. The player was a sideshow feature named Harold Smith: bannerline billing, simply Musical Harold. No Professor, Maestro, Signor or even Duke or Prince. Disappointing. And also Harold didn't perform in some bizarre custume, just wore a rumpled dark-gray tuxedo with snap-on bow tie. He could have been a waiter with tired feet in some down-in-the-mouth New York west side bistro. I found Harold shy, quiet, self-effacing. Medium tall and thin, bony-faced, with shoulders slightly hunched — likely from so much bending over those beloved tuned glasses.

"I got the idea for playing musical glasses when I was a boy," Harold told me. I saw a man at the old Hippodrome playing glasses by hitting them with a mallet. I tried it on the glasses at home, but found I could get a sweeter tone by rubbing the rims with a wet finger."

Before he played Harold always washed his hands thoroughly, rinsed off the soap, and kept his hands wet while playing. Also, the glasses had to be spotlessly clean. He owned more than 300 crystal glasses and used 40 in performances, covering about three octaves and placed in chromatic sequence. The more water, the lower the note, because vibrations of the water-free glass surface are what make the notes. The more dry surface that there is to vibrate, the higher the response of the note.

Waltzes sound best on the glasses. In fast numbers Harold barely had time to touch the rims and therefore they didn't produce really pleasant tones. His ambition was to put together a musical-glasses quintet with several hundred glasses and attempt to play symphonic music. He was never able to pull off such a musical marvel.

Mozart performed on musical glasses. Both he and Beethoven wrote music for them. Mozart's best compositions for the tuned glasses were the Adagio, K, 616a, written in the last year of his life, 1791, and an Adagio and Rondo, K617, with cello, flute, oboe, and viola. Gaetano Donizetti,

MUSICAL HAROLD

the celebrated Italian composer, wrote a part for the glass harmonium in Lucia's mad scene in *Lucia di Lammermoor*, the alternate instrument being the flute.

The music of massaged glasses turned up in fairly modern times with the 1919 opera, *Die Frau ohne Schatten* by Richard Strauss of Munich. George Crumb, an American composer, born in 1929, revived the weird musical instrument in the last movement of his 1970 electric string quartet, *Black Angels*. In Germany today there is a virtuoso of musical glasses, Bruno Hoffman, who plays the old original way with fingers rotating on glasses' rims, claiming it adds subtety to his playing.

Harold Smith knew of only two modern musical glasses virtuosi: a man named Turner ("He's *great!*") and a girl, whom he's seen on television's "Late Night with David Letterman." ("She don't seem to hold the notes and jumps around too much," was the appraisal of musical-glasses pioneer, Harold Smith.")—*B.B.*

"Here will we sit and let the sounds of music
Creep in our ears; soft stillness and the night
Become the touches of sweet harmony."

William Shakespeare (1564–1616)
The Merchant of Venice 1596–97

THE ACCORDION

The accordion's ancestor: an 1100 B.C. Chinese instrument, the *sheng*, brought by Italian missionaries to Europe in the 18th century. First Western name: the *handaoline*; became accordion in 1829, a peoples' instrument, popular in cafes, dance halls, street festivals, weddings, and *bar mitzvahs*. In the mid-1950s squeeze-box virtuoso turned the "Lady of Spain" into a schmaltzy street walker. After ten years of glib ear-torturing, the accordion was attacked by the guitar, spearheaded by the advent of the Beatles. But now it is making a recovery as people glance back to their ethnic roots and lovers and promoters of the accordion start to develop legit literature for their much-abused and hackneyed accordion. — *B.B.*

Social-political painter Ben Shahn's sad and biting comment on the death of President Franklin Delano Roosevelt. A blind accordionist pays tribute along the route of the funeral cortege.

"Hands make perfect portraits.
You are the only one with your hands."

Adapted from *The Blind Accordion Player* by
Ben Shahn. Owner: Mr. & Mrs. Roy R.
Neuberger

Bernard Korman
American taxi driver, artist: NYC
He sketches hands of passengers
who are not in a hurry.

Edith Piaf Meets Her Idol, Charlie Chaplin

"Chaplin is not a great lover of night-life . . . certainly not a fan of cabaret . . . and when they told me that he was sitting out there near the stage, I knew that this was to be the special occasion I had wished for, albeit unconsciously, for a long time.

"That evening strangely enough I did not get my usual stage fight. I'd never met Charlie Chaplin but seen his films time and again, enough to reassure me. I could look upon him as a friend. My voice might not overwhelm him but there would be a bond of understanding between us.

"Never before or since have I sung so well. I had to make my singing say 'thank you' for the moments of intense feeling he had given me. This little fellow he created has made me laugh because Charlie planned it that way. Through him came courage and hope.

"After the show Chaplin told me that my singing had touched him in a way few singers had done. A precious compliment, yet I found myself tongue-tied. I just blushed and spluttered. Later, I was absolutely furious with myself. I was astonished when, the next day, Chaplin telephoned and invited me to visit him the following day at his house in Beverly Hills. I was not expected until after lunch. I had a wonderful time there. Charlie is most unpretentious, his conversation delightful, his voice pleasant — a certain timidity about him. He put me at ease by recalling his music-hall days in the Fred Karno act. Later he spoke about France. He loves France: 'Not only,' he said, 'because the French have always appreciated my films, but because to me the country epitomizes gentleness and freedom.' He played some of his own compositions on the violin. I was so happy to have met him and found him just as I had imagined.

" 'Edith,' he said, as I got into the car to go home, 'one day I'll write a song for you, words and music.' "

Edith Piaf (1915–1963)
French cabaret singer.
The Wheel of Fortune autobiography 1958
English translation: Peter Owen

Charlie Chaplin Visits a Hollywood Night Club

"This was apparently the first time in many months that he had taken Paulette [Goddard] to a nightclub, and she came alive and shining at the prospect of breaking with some regularity out of the Chaplin cloister-on-the-hill into the high life. If that's was what was on her mind, she soon was dismally disillusioned.

"The midnight show at the Coconut Grove was coming to its end in the usual melancholy atmosphere of reeking smoke, flat champagne, and lovers staring at the table and having second thoughts. The star performer was one Gene Austin, a sugary crooner who modulated his final notes a whole octave higher and so gave out the sound of a boy soprano or castrato. 'Revolting,' muttered Chaplin, who had declined into a brooding silence. Riding home, Paulette kept up the heart-breaking pretense that from now on her evenings would be agog with music and dancing. Chaplin gave her a black parental look. He started in about the cacophony of jazz, which he hated, and went on about the decadence of night life, the excruciating 'eunuch' sounds to which we had been subjected, and the fate, similar to that of Sodom, which would shortly overtake the Republic. Paulette saw her vision collapse like the ghost of Christmas Present. A tear ran down her enchanting face and her eyes fairly popped in frustration as she said, 'What are we going to do evenings — *stay home and write theses?!*' Well, Chaplin replied, 'One night a year is enough of that rubbish.' "

Alistair Cooke
  English journalist.
  Six Men 1977 . . . "Charles Chaplin,
  The One and Only."

CHARLIE CHAPLIN talks about his music

"I tried to compose elegant and romantic music to frame my comedies in contrast to the tramp character for elegant music gave my comedies an emotional dimension. Musical arrangers rarely understood this. They wanted the music to be funny. But I would explain that I wanted no competition. I wanted the music to be a counterpoint of grace and charm, to express sentiment, without which, as Hazlitt says, a work of art is incomplete."

Charles Spencer Chaplin (1889–1977)
My Autobiography 1964.

Drawing adapted from
Photoplay Magazine
Paper Dolls by Percy Reeves 1918

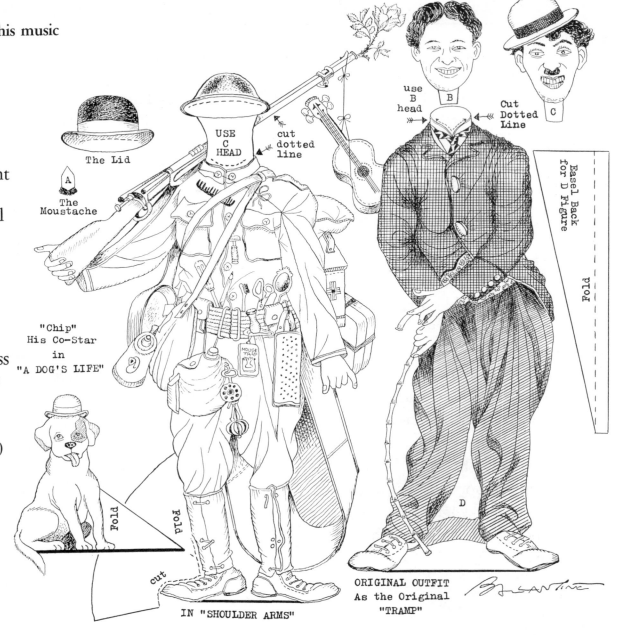

The Lid

A
The
Moustache

USE
C
HEAD

cut
dotted
line

"Chip"
His Co-Star
in
"A DOG'S LIFE"

Fold

Fold

cut

IN "SHOULDER ARMS"

use
B
head

B

Cut
Dotted
Line

C

Easel Back
for D Figure

Fold

D

ORIGINAL OUTFIT
As the Original
"TRAMP"

AGONIES OF MUSICIANS

Young professional musicians are beginning to worry about their budding careers suddenly ending due to worrisome agonies creeping into their seemingly healthy bodies: niggling ailments that become difficult to shrug off. Doctors call the problem an "overuse syndrome."

Continual practicing causes tendons to press on nerves. Ice packs and towel wraps seem not to offer much relief. Scores of aggravations menace musicians' well-being. Some maladies are minor irritations that come and go, but other problems are capable of chopping off promising careers. Among musical bogeys are carpal-tunnel syndrome and debilitating hand cramps that have finished off such fine pianists as Gary Graffman and Leon Fleisher. The list of threatening ailments is long: back pain and tendonitis among pianists and string players; sore tongues, bruised lips and an assortment of mouth problems affect wind players. There are sore shoulders and cramps for drummers, cymbalists, and conductors. Sternums of cellists take a beating. Ears and tongues of bassoonists pay a price for playing that wind-demander. Stress of mastering big brasses — tubas, flugel horn, euphonium — can bring on hernias. Symphony players get hemorrhoids from long periods of sitting. Guitar players get sore nipples from pressure to their chests.

Locations of these ailments are indicated on a peculiar (to say the least) medical chart on the next page. In a sidebar following this serious report, Dr. Paulisch bares all about the photo portrait on which the drawing is based.

Music medicine has just begun to be effective, taking a rightful place alongside sports medicine, though an analogy with that branch of medical mending may be misleading, as musical patients, while well-compensated, are not usually well-heeled. Most are students or young professionals without generous backers. Very little financial pressure is being exerted to find medical solutions for the aggravating ailments. However, two major U.S. cities have set up informal clinics of doctors with varying specialties to diagnose and treat afflicted musicians. The findings suggest that two-thirds of pro musicians suffer physical problems related to their work, and that 20 percent are serious enough to affect performances. Together those clinics treat about 700 musicians annually: in Cleveland, over 200, in Boston over 500.

Many doctors who treat musicians play instruments themselves. The importance of treating a player by another player is understood when we know that even the slightest change in placement of a tooth — as little as one-thousandth of an inch — can be disastrous to a wind player's *embouchure*. — B.B.

A G O N I E S of M U S I C I A N S

Musicians often are the cause of their problems. Many develop when the best-possible playing techniques are not being used. Some players prepare for auditions or concerts by practicing without letup — no stretchings, no relaxing breaks, no icing of muscles or joints that may stiffen.

Stress of performance is another troublesome factor. Studies show that performance increases musicians' pulse rate by almost 90 percent. An experiment made on a trombone soloist of a major symphony orchestra showed that his average pulse rate of 75 beats per minute jumped to 230 during his stellar trombone solo in Ravel's *Bolero*. Musical performers call such performance anxiety "soloist heartthrob" instead of stage fright.

The International Conference of Symphony and Opera Musicians, concerned about the extent of musicians' medical problems, made a survey of its 48-member orchestras.

"At this point," says ICSOM president, Melanie Burrell, "we don't know professionally the extent of our medical problems; we just know that they're there."

Burrell, a cellist in the Denver, Colorado, symphony, has been treated for tendonitis and had operations on both her hands.

Dr. Paulisch's Strange Chart's Photo

'Got it from a guy who'd got it at auction in a small Pennsylvania town. Mamieville. Never heard of it, and I'm native Keystoner. He said it's of a local kook name of Ellsworth Chinotsky. Wrote it all down on the back. Trumpet player for the Salvation Army in Pittsburgh, downriver a bit. Elzy was stagestruck. Run away once to Broadway to get into vaudeville. Got to the Flatiron Building, was picked up and fetched home. Later, Elzy was conned by the local volunteer firemen to star in their annual stag smoker banquet at the Liederkranz Hall. Theme that year was 'The Garden of Eden.' Elzy was Adam, with a genuine fig leaf sent up from Florida by an uncle. Eve was Veronica Winesap, a favorite floozie exotic from Curly Laycock's *Venetian Moon*, down by the brewery. At midnight she popped up in the buff out of a giant apple strudel concocted at Weisenheimmer's German Bakery. Sweet success with a tart ending. Mrs. Lotz, who lived next door to the music hall, had stood on a chair up in her attic to peek over the tops of scenery flats leaned against the ballroom's high windows to frustrate peeping toms. She reported the shocking tableau to the Irish parish priest. Wrathfully, he closed the song club and its bar for a month in punishment of indignant exposure. And that's about all I know about it."

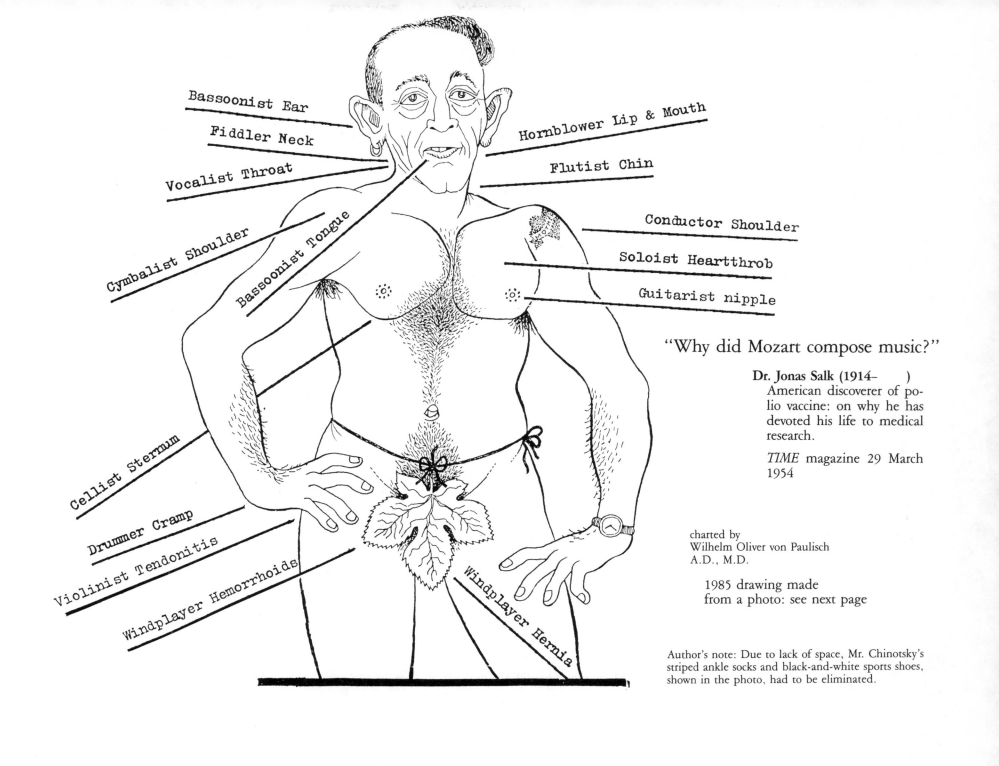

Bassoonist Ear

Fiddler Neck

Vocalist Throat

Cymbalist Shoulder

Bassoonist Tongue

Hornblower Lip & Mouth

Flutist Chin

Conductor Shoulder

Soloist Heartthrob

Guitarist nipple

Cellist Sternum

Drummer Cramp

Violinist Tendonitis

Windplayer Hemorrhoids

Windplayer Hernia

"Why did Mozart compose music?"

Dr. Jonas Salk (1914–   )
American discoverer of polio vaccine: on why he has devoted his life to medical research.

TIME magazine 29 March 1954

charted by
Wilhelm Oliver von Paulisch
A.D., M.D.

1985 drawing made
from a photo: see next page

Author's note: Due to lack of space, Mr. Chinotsky's striped ankle socks and black-and-white sports shoes, shown in the photo, had to be eliminated.

curtain speech

"I never took one of Bement's classes at
Columbia University, but one day walking down
the hall I heard music from his classroom. Being
curious I opened the door and went in. A
low-toned record was being played and the students
were asked to make a drawing from what they
heard. So I sat down and made a drawing too.
Then he played a very different kind of record — a
sort of high soprano piece — for another quick
drawing. This gave me an idea that I was very
interested to follow later — the idea that music
could be transplanted into something for the eye."

Georgia O'Keeffe **(1887–1986)**
American painter

Georgia O'Keefe, A Studio Book 1976

"One never knows, do one?"

Thomas "Fats" Waller
    American jazz pianist, vocalist, composer
    His favorite expression on all occasions.

"I have ventured,
Like little wanton boys that swim on bladders,
This many summers in a sea of glory,
But far beyond my depth."

William Shakespeare
  English poet, player, playwright.
  i. Henry VI I.ii.